HOW TO START A BUSINESS WHEN YOU'RE YOUNG

D0683291

HOW TO START A BUSINESS WHEN YOU'RE YOUNG

Get the right idea for success

BARRIE HAWKINS AND LUKE WING

A&C Black • London

First published in Great Britain 2009

2 | 2

A & C Black Publishers Ltd
36 Soho Square, London W1D 3QY
www.acblack.com

Copyright © Barrie Hawkins and Luke Wing, 2009

A CIP record for this book is available from the British Library.

ISBN: 9-781-4081-1110-9

This book is produced using paper that is made from wood grown in managed, sustainable forests. It is natural, renewable and recyclable. The logging and manufacturing processes conform to the environmental regulations of the country of origin.

Design by Fiona Pike, Pike Design, Winchester
Typeset by Saxon Graphics Ltd, Derby
Printed in the United Kingdom by Cox & Wyman, Reading RG1 8EX

This book is dedicated to Angela Gilburn,
whose help and support is really appreciated.

AUTHORS' NOTE

SOME WORDS OF CAUTION

The aim of *How to Start a Business When You're Young* is to help you generate an idea for a new business and then to set up and establish that business. Although we hope you'll come up with lots of exciting possibilities, neither we – the authors – nor the publishers can be held responsible for the viability of any ideas you come up with, or the business ideas referred to in the book. Before incurring any obligations, seek professional advice and thoroughly evaluate your proposal.

CONTENTS

APPENDICES

PART ONE:
HOW TO GET THE IDEA

CHAPTER 1
NOTHING IS
STOPPING YOU

Most people, after leaving school or college or university, get a job and spend the rest of their lives working for somebody else.

But you're not most people.

The fact that you've picked up this book and started to read it shows that you're at least willing to consider the possibility of not going down the same route the mass of people go down. *You* could be your own boss. *You* could have all the benefits that come with that.

However...let's pause there for a moment. We want this book to inspire and motivate you. Over the last 15 years or so, Barrie has worked with thousands of people who wanted to set up and run their own business, while Luke has recently taken that big step and is now running his business. Drawing on our combined experiences, we'll show you how you could go about this, but we want your ambitions to be built on a solid foundation. So, straightaway, let's make it clear: running your own business does, of course, carry responsibilities – you're the boss, so you have to make the decisions.

Also, we can tell you that most people have the wrong notion about what is needed to start a business and build it up to be a success. Talk to people who haven't got their own business, and they'll spout all kinds of nonsense, misconceptions and wrong opinions.

Worse still, as someone who's not in your 40s or 50s or 60s, you're likely to hear loads of drivel from people who are – stuff, for example, about lack of business experience.

Yes, there are hurdles to overcome, but we're going to show you ways around the usual ones. We'll look at plenty of real-life examples of what others have done to build a successful business – and none of these people are sporting a grey beard or even middle-age spread.

'You need a brilliant business idea'

No you don't. When you tell people what your business idea is, don't worry if you don't get the response: 'Wow, what a terrific idea! Wish I'd thought of that!'

You don't *need* that sort of idea and that sort of response. If you do come up with something that's really different from what's out there now, then well done, but it certainly isn't essential.

Experience has taught us that the more unusual your idea, the harder it can be to get it off the ground because it can take people – customers – a long time to understand it or to get used to something that's very different.

So it's not necessary for other people to be massively impressed with the idea you come up with for starting a business. After working with countless successful business start-ups, we can tell you that your idea has to meet two criteria, outlined below, neither of which requires it to be a 'brilliant' idea, whatever that means.

Firstly, the idea for a product or service has to work in the marketplace; in other words people have to want or need to buy the product or service. There are billions of people in the world, and millions of businesses and organisations, and they all need products and services, so coming up with something that some of those people, businesses and organisations need is not the most challenging part.

Secondly, most people setting up in business overlook one important factor: not only does their idea have to work in the marketplace, but it should also be something that *suits them*. When you are your own boss, you don't have a manager or a supervisor checking their watch if you arrive a few minutes late on a Monday morning. Your business has to be something that makes you get out of bed on Monday morning not because you'll get a rollocking if you're late, but because you *want* to – because you enjoy what you do, you like running your own business. Yes, you like the money you earn, but you could earn money in any boring job, whereas success will come much more easily if you spend your days doing something that suits your personality, suits your skills, suits your interests, suits your ambitions.

So, ideally, to start up a successful business, you need a tailor-made business idea. And *How to Start a Business When You're Young* is going to help you come up with that idea.

'You need lots of money to start a business'

No, you don't *need* thousands and thousands of pounds to start a business. Some business ideas do require a lot of capital to start, but that doesn't mean you need a lot of capital to start *your* business. Many types of businesses can be started with very little or almost no money. For example, you might be able to provide a service using some skill or knowledge you already possess.

Or if you came up with an idea that did require considerable investment, then a way round it could be not to give up on the idea completely, but to come up with another idea that didn't require a big investment – the techniques revealed in this book will help you to do this – then use some of the profits from the low-cost start-up to invest in your big idea later.

Alternatively, if you came up with a really original idea for a product, maybe you could ask an existing manufacturer with the means to do the development and marketing work to take it on for you and pay you a royalty – a percentage of the profits – on every item sold. If you have the motivation, the desire, the ambition, the dream, you can always find ways around what appears to be an obstacle. For young people in particular, there are various schemes and assistance available, such as grants, to help you finance your start-up.

'You have to have paper qualifications to run your own business'

Not true. Some of the most famous and successful entrepreneurs running business empires today didn't shine in academic subjects at school. Failing your history or English literature exam is no bar to setting up and running a successful business. If this is you, look at what other subjects you're interested in. Some of these may be of a practical nature, showing you've got skills or talents that *would* help you in business. For example, if you're good at sport, you probably have a competitive side to your nature and will enjoy that aspect of business: watching the competition and working out how to beat them at their own game. Or perhaps you enjoy team sports in particular, making you a good team player, which would also be an asset in business. Start a business that grows and you will soon be working with other people, not just employees, but possibly business partners.

Working through this book will give you a solid grounding in what you need to know to start and grow a successful business. Today there is probably more help available than ever before for young entrepreneurs. Successive governments have been keen to encourage young people to consider the possibility of having their own business. There is a lot of help available through organisations such as Business Link (**www.businesslink.gov.uk**), a government-funded national business support network; local enterprise agencies which specialise in helping new businesses; and the Prince's Trust youth charity (**www.princes-trust.org.uk**). The type of support offered includes courses and one-to-one advice sessions with experienced business counsellors and virtually all of this help is free. We'll look at these later in the book but, for now, remember:

you don't have to be an Einstein at exams to build yourself a future with your own business.

'You don't have any business experience'

Nor did Barrie when he started his first business, nor did Luke when he started his first business.

Actually, that's not strictly true. We each of us had some business experience, the same experience that you have – as a customer.

As a customer of products and services, you know what people expect, what people want. You know how you like to be treated as a customer. Indeed, you have special knowledge as a customer: you know what *young* people want and like. So that gives you an advantage over the 40 year olds who are trying to start a business for a product or service where the customers will include people in your age group.

In any case, many middle-aged and older people who set up a business don't have business experience either. Perhaps they have always worked for the government, or local government, or a government-funded organisation, or a not-for-profit organisation, or a charity. And the fact that you've not spent years working in somebody else's business might even work to your advantage. Some hugely successful entrepreneurs have succeeded precisely because they've not done things in the same way as other people before them; they haven't followed the conventional route.

So if other people tell you that you don't have the benefit of lots of business experience – or life experience – tell them about the *advantages* you do have in starting a business at your age. Lots of people in their 30s and 40s, tired of the routine or the boredom of their jobs, dream of starting their own business, but by then they may have big responsibilities: big mortgage, three or four kids, lots of credit agreements. Starting a business before you have all these responsibilities gives you a degree of freedom and flexibility. You'll have less pressure – too much pressure can mean you're not working at your best. Also, you'll have more time to devote to your business. OK, you want to go out and enjoy yourself, but right now you probably don't have the demands on your time that you'll have later, such as having to pick up the kids from school every day and then drop them off at ballet class, or whatever. And as some people get older, they get jaded. The experience of working for other people – routine, bosses who are not up to the job, unfulfilling work – can drain away enthusiasm and ambition and expectations and hopes. You've got a reservoir of energy and enthusiasm and drive.

Get out there. The world is waiting.

CHAPTER 2
YOUR FUTURE, YOUR BUSINESS

A recent survey revealed that most people would like to have their own business – 60 per cent of the UK population in fact. But, for most of these, it will remain just a dream. Because a business starts with a business idea and most people never come up with the right idea.

So the first part of *How to Start a Business When You're Young* is dedicated to helping *you* come up with the right idea to start *your* business. Or perhaps you already have an idea and are tempted to skip Part One of the book, in which case hold on a minute. The next few chapters will reveal a whole range of approaches and techniques you can use to generate ideas for a business, tools which have been used by others before you to come up with ideas that have worked brilliantly for them, so you might come up with an even better idea than the one you have now. If you're thinking that's not possible, our response is: you can always come up with a better idea once you know how to do it.

A word of caution: beware of falling head over heels in love with one particular idea. Even if friends and family have told you what a terrific idea it is, think again. Experience tells us that when you come to assess whether it will actually work, when you go through the process of evaluation that we'll look at later in the book, you might discover some obstacle that makes you think it would be better to try another idea. If you've allowed yourself to become besotted with just one idea and only worked on that solitary idea, and then the time comes when you decide it's not for you, the level of disappointment you'll face in having to give up on your one idea might deflate you. Far safer to be working on two or three ideas, or even a handful, until one rises to the top as being the most promising.

And if that doesn't convince you, consider this before you devote all your energies to one solitary idea: what exactly is it you want from having your own business? In being your own boss, what are the benefits you are seeking?

A common misconception about business start-ups is that having your own business, being your own boss, is only about making money. Of course we all want to make money – we all have to pay the bills and we all want to have cash left over to enjoy ourselves. But it's not solely about that and nothing else. There are many reasons why people start a business and all kinds of benefits that they are looking for and hoping it will bring them.

What *you* want from your business will depend on your interests, your personality, your ambitions, your home circumstances and your financial circumstances. The clearer you are about what you want from having your own business, the more likely it is you'll achieve it. Hazy ambitions and goals lead to hazy, unsatisfying, results.

So if you're thinking of setting up your own business, the first thing you need to know is WHY? To help you discover exactly what it is you might be seeking, we'll together go through some possibilities. As we work through the possibilities, just pause and ask yourself: is this something that applies to me? Is this something I'd want from having my own business? If the answer is yes, then put a tick on the dotted line provided. These possible benefits are numbered 1 to 10. At the end of this chapter you'll find two blank boxes for you to fill in: when you finish working your way through the possibilities, go back over the list and write down in Box A the number that relates to each benefit you have ticked.

There's no way that all of these possibilities will apply to you, since some of them are contradictory. Hopefully, though, you will end up with a handful of numbers in that box.

Work your way through these possibilities and you'll find they'll help shape your business idea, pointing towards what you could consider and ruling out other ideas.

1. Doing something for yourself ....
We can't describe this better than *Hayley* did. Hayley came on to our business start-up course aged 23, having left school at 16 and

undertaken a secretarial course before starting her first full-time job at 17. In the next five years, she had five different jobs.

Hayley told us: 'I'm fed up with spending my days working for other people so they can afford the things I can't.'

Does that strike a chord with you? If so, put a tick on the dotted line above and write the number '1' in Box A on page 20.

2. Prove there is a better way of doing things   ....

You might think that the prime motivation for setting up a business is to do something for yourself, but having met thousands of would-be entrepreneurs we've discovered this is not always so. Here's an example of what for some people is a major driving force:

'I really don't like the way they do things at work, the way they treat their customers, the way they treat their staff, even their suppliers. I feel there must be a better way of doing it and I want to set up my own business to prove that there is.'

That was *Alex*, who felt compelled to start his own business three years after leaving university. Once a new graduate with high ideals and high standards, he'd rapidly been disillusioned with what he experienced in the world of employment outside university.

Does proving there is a better way of doing things appeal to you? If so, tick on the dotted line above and enter '2' in Box A on page 20.

You'll notice that, in what we're doing here, the emphasis is very much on motivation. One of the earliest lessons we learned from working with people on our business start-up course was the importance of finding out what motivated them. The satisfaction you get from doing something that motivates you can be a huge benefit of having your own business. If we can help you locate the right motivation buttons to push, it will unleash huge volumes of energy and enthusiasm. This asset – being fired up with motivation – also extends to people in other fields. Take sport, for example. Sporting champions are motivated to practise and train beyond the level of those individuals lacking the same drive and energy, who aren't fuelled by high levels of motivation. Without doubt, the more motivation you have, the more likely it is that your business will succeed.

3. Demonstrate what you are capable of   ....

Are you sure you've shown the world what you are capable of? If school, with its emphasis on studying and paper qualifications, didn't suit you, then up to now you have spent a large part of your life in an environment that has not brought out the best in you. Or, even if you are brilliant at scholarly subjects, you'll have other skills and qualities that you haven't yet exploited to the full. Setting up your own business is going to be your chance to make full use of untapped or underused qualities and abilities.

Mel, 17, told us: 'I want to show my mum and dad that I'm capable of doing something more than taking the dog for a walk.'

Launching and building up your own successful business could give you a sense of achievement, a level of achievement you haven't yet experienced, even if you've done well in other fields. You will be able to look back and say 'I did this.'

4. Being financially independent   ....

OK, let's talk about money now. You might be surprised to learn that, in our experience, the majority of people setting up in business are not looking for great wealth. Most are looking for financial independence, by which we mean the ability to pay the bills, not just today but for the foreseeable future. We all know, today, there's no such thing as a job for life: if in the future you're made redundant you'll find your employers have pulled the financial rug out from under you and suddenly cut off your source of income. That happened to co-author Barrie. He set up his own business after being made redundant and finding himself unemployed for four months. He'd had his career mapped out ahead of him, or so he thought, then all of a sudden he received this letter in a brown envelope. Without a salary, the savings soon ran out. He resolved that would never happen to him again.

Apart from the help this book gives you, we hope you'll be taking up the opportunities offered by organisations such as Business Link and the Prince's Trust. Quite properly, they will warn you about the element of risk involved in setting up your own enterprise. Our own view is that, in one sense, it's not as risky as it used to be because the alternative – having a job – is not as safe as it used to be.

And look at it this way: when you're trying to find a job, you are in effect a salesperson. What you are selling is your labour. If you get a job, you've found a customer for your labour. But just the one customer. If that customer cancels, you're in trouble. But when you work for yourself, running your own business, you can have as many customers as you can get.

5. Become a millionaire ....

Who wants to be rich? Don't be shy about ticking number 5 and putting it in the box – if you have big ambitions, put it down.

Realistically, aiming for something you hope will bring such high rewards probably does entail a higher element of risk. When Barrie decided to set up his business start-up courses, nobody said to him: 'Wow! That's a terrific idea. Wish I'd thought of that.' His idea lacked the 'wow' factor. Indeed, quite a few friends pointed out that there were already a lot of suppliers of start-up training (to which his reaction was: 'Then there must be a market for it'). Running a business that helps other people to set up their own business is unlikely ever to see him riding about in a new Rolls-Royce, but having lost his job and his income, his prime aim was to avoid that situation recurring. So he wanted to set up a business where there was a steady demand, a demand that was unlikely to disappear overnight.

Barrie's story demonstrates why we're trying to bring out what it is that you are looking for in having your own business. His own case illustrates how the benefit you want from having the business shapes the business idea: he wanted long-term security of income, to be financially independent, and that took precedence over any hopes he might have had of great wealth. So what level of income do you want?

6. An outlet for your creativity ....

You have a creative side to you: maybe you are good at coming up with ideas or have some kind of artistic ability, or perhaps you've a talent for a particular craft activity? If you're shaking your head while reading this, then what that tells us is not that you don't have creative ability but that you haven't yet discovered it. Or perhaps you are creative in some way but up to now you haven't had a chance to use it to the full.

If you can tap into your creativity, it will give you and your business two advantages over other people and other businesses. Firstly, if you don't use your creative ability, you may feel unfulfilled, even frustrated, so setting up a business that explores your creativity can be liberating and energising. Secondly, exploring and utilising your unique creative ability will give your business a benefit that the competition doesn't have.

7. Spending your days doing something you enjoy   ....

At your age it's possible that you've been very lucky up to now and never had a job, either part-time or full-time, that was boring. Maybe that is yet to come – unless you start your own business!

Jason had endured four years of working for a government department before he could stand it no longer and came on to our business start-up course. He told us he had a calendar pinned up on the wall in front of his desk: at lunchtime and at the end of the day he would mark off another half day gone until the weekend came. He lived for Saturdays and Sundays. But even his weekends were spoilt: from Sunday lunchtime onwards he started to get a sinking feeling as Monday morning approached. We told him: 'This is your life you are marking off on this calendar.'

So how about spending your days doing something you find absorbing and enjoyable? Have you a hobby or interest that you could turn into a business? This has been the route taken by hundreds of people setting up their own business.

8. More time for yourself   ....

If you currently have a full-time job, perhaps this would appeal to you: working less.

Another popular misconception about running your own business is that you have to work long hours. Certainly, today lots of *employees* work very long hours. Indeed, often the higher you go up the corporate ladder the more hours you have to put in. You may be surprised to know that on our business start-up course we enrol many successful professional people, including lawyers, doctors and stockbrokers. *Philippa*, who at 24 had only recently qualified as a solicitor, told us it was common for ambitious young lawyers in her firm to still be in the office at eight o'clock at night.

It's true that many people who run their own business work what you and we might regard as long hours, but very often this is because they really enjoy what they're doing and they get so much satisfaction from the work itself or from building up a successful business. Remember, in building up a business, you're not just earning money to pay the bills that month, you are building up a valuable asset that you might want to sell in the future. And many people running their own successful business are willing to put in extra effort now so they can retire early. But if a long day is not for you, you must choose the right business idea.

Barrie confesses he doesn't work full-time. Actually, to be more accurate, he doesn't work full-time at something that provides him with an income. For part of the week he does voluntary work, as the unpaid chairman of a specialist animal welfare society. The society rescues and re-homes German Shepherd dogs. You may not share Barrie's passion for rescuing homeless or ill-treated dogs, but it's possible that there's something that matters to you, something you'd like to spend time doing. Think about this. Is there some cause dear to your heart? Perhaps you're interested in conservation or alleviating poverty or some other good causes?

Would you like to be able to devote some of your time to that? Once you get on the nine to five-thirty treadmill five days a week – or perhaps you're already on it – you may find there's not enough time at weekends to do all you want, especially when you take on life's little commitments, such as kids.

Or maybe there's something you'd like to do for yourself. Build a racing car? Play in a band? Write a novel? You could come up with a business idea where each week you devoted half a day, or a whole day, maybe even more, to something other than earning a living.

The brilliant news is that in cutting your working hours you might not lose as much of your income as you'd expect. That's because it is the top slice of your income which bears the heaviest burden of tax, so you might find, for example, that you work 20 per cent less but only lose 10 or 15 per cent of your income.

The benefit of perhaps working fewer hours is closely allied to the next possibility.

9. Flexibility   ....
Today, more and more people are demanding greater flexibility in their working lives. That is partly due to changes in our society. For instance, increasing numbers of people starting their own business require some flexibility in their lives because they are single parents. And plenty of those single parents are in your age group.

This is a good example of how thinking about the benefits you want from having your own business will help to shape the business idea. And how your personality and your likes and dislikes need to be taken into account. Perhaps the same routine, the same place every day, the same faces, simply doesn't appeal to you? If so, then maybe you shouldn't launch that take-away food outlet in the high street, open from 11 a.m. to 11 p.m. seven days a week, which due to financial limitations is staffed mostly by you.

Perhaps it would suit you to work, say, mornings and evenings, or to work on a Saturday and take a day off in the week? What are your particular needs and what appeals to you? Come up with the right business idea and you could have that flexibility.

10. A challenge   ....
We've deliberately left this one until last. Would you like an injection of excitement in your life?

As we've seen, it's possible to choose a fairly safe business idea, one where the risks involved are fairly small. Indeed, there is such a thing as a 'business in a box'. This is a business that supplies a product or service for which there is a popular demand; you track down an established trade supplier with a track record and you sell that product or service. It almost certainly wouldn't have the 'wow' factor we mentioned earlier, but taking this route could see you set up in business within a matter of weeks.

But maybe that's not for you. Perhaps you're ready for a bigger challenge? Is it time for a bit of excitement in your life, even a bit of risk? This might take the form of a brand-new product or service, something unlike anything else. Would you be prepared to take big risks – if the potential rewards were big enough?

You choose. It's your life. It's your future. It's your business.

BOX A   Which of the above possible benefits appeal to you? Write down the numbers here:

BOX B   Are there any other benefits you would like in having your
own business?

Write them down here:

CHAPTER 3
YOUR STARTING POINT

A business starts with a business idea, but in our experience most people who are trying to come up with an idea for a business go about it the wrong way.

Many times we've heard people say: 'I lay awake at night tossing and turning, trying to think of what business I could start.'

Trying to pluck ideas out of the air like that is not the most productive way to come up with an idea for a business. Instead, the following chapters will reveal a whole range of techniques and approaches you can use to generate ideas. They will give you some guidance in your efforts to come up with an idea and stimulate your thinking.

To achieve these aims we'll use two different methods: some of what we do will involve you in the gathering of valuable information which you then use to generate ideas; we'll also employ creative techniques that will help you come up with an idea that is new to you or new to the area where you are setting up in business, or even a completely original idea that no-one else has yet tried.

You will of course need somewhere to record the business ideas as they come to you. If you wish, use our *Record of business ideas* in Appendix 1 at the back of the book. So, for example, if while reading Chapter 6 on coming up with ideas for new products you have a sudden flash of inspiration, you can make a note of this in the section for Chapter 6 of the *Record*.

Let's gets started on this search for a business idea. The starting point has to be YOU.

You need to draw out and put under the spotlight your capabilities, your experience, your personality, your interests. Put all these together and it makes a unique combination. There is no-one else quite like you. Being fully aware of your capabilities and experience can help point you towards a tailor-made business idea. One that suits you.

We've already begun this path of discovery, by getting you to reveal what you want from your own business.

To help get you thinking about who you are, what you know and what you can do, we'll set down some questions. We'll also give some guidance on answering them. You can record your answers in the *Who am I?* questionnaire, which you'll find in Appendix 2.

At this point, you may be getting the impression that coming up with a business idea is going to involve a lot of written work. If so, we are giving you a false impression. It's important to keep a record of the ideas you come up with as you go along, so that you don't forget them, and also to record some of the useful information you've gathered because you may be coming back and using it time and time again. But as we go through the tools, techniques and approaches for coming up with ideas you'll see that the emphasis is mostly on practical things for you to go away and do. So, even if writing isn't your strong point, it's worth making this early effort because the benefits you might get in the end will be so great. And it's only here at the beginning, where we're sorting things out so that your time will be spent efficiently, that there is more writing than doing.

WHO AM I?

It's up to you whether you want to read through all the questions in our guidance notes here before setting down your answers in the questionnaire in Appendix 2. You may prefer to deal with them one at a time, reading the question and our notes on it and then filling in your answer in the Appendix.

1. What sort of business would you LIKE to run?

We've started with a really broad question.

One important matter you should immediately give thought to is whether you have a preference for a business that revolves around products or one that provides a service. With a product-based business you have a physical product for customers to see and try, whereas with a service, such as a cleaning service, customers have to trust that you'll provide what you say you will. So, many business consultants will tell you that it may be easier to sell a product than a service.

Perhaps you're simply more interested in selling a product than providing a service. Maybe there's a type of product you like and know quite a lot about. For example, *Amanda*, who came on to our course while she was studying full-time at college and was looking to set up a part-time business, loved jewellery. She took a stall on her local crafts market on Saturdays, offering just earrings, but the biggest range of earrings most of her customers had ever seen. So if you're keen on or have particular knowledge of a certain product, then this could be the direction you choose to take.

It's probably true to say that if your product were to take off, it would be easier to expand the business. If you wanted to expand a service-based business, you'd have to recruit more staff and train them. And with a service business you are of course relying on the people you employ, so it can be harder to control and maintain quality: the mechanic you employ might have a cold that day – or a hangover – and not be working to the best of his or her ability.

Think of other ways in which people might affect the sort of business you'd like to run. Do you like meeting people face-to-face? Or would you be happier running a traditional mail-order business or a business on eBay? Running a premises-based business might not appeal if you like to be out and about, or if you like to be always meeting new faces. What if your business was one which involved you in staying away from home? For instance, there might be few buyers for the type of product or service you are offering and so you could spend much of your time travelling

in the UK – or abroad – staying in hotels. How will your boyfriend/
girlfriend back home feel about that?

And would you like to run a business where you had to make
formal sales presentations to groups of people? That might seem
only a small consideration, but public speaking can be a frightening
prospect for many people. Still, if you really liked the business idea,
you could always enrol on a course to improve your public-
speaking skills: the ability to speak in public is a valuable asset for
anyone running their own business. As soon as your new business
got off the ground you could give talks to local organisations about
the joys and challenges of starting a business when you're young
– and there might be potential customers in the audience.

And when it comes to customers, are you a 'hunter'? Are you
the sort of character who relishes the thought of going out every
week and searching out new customers? If you're in business,
you're in the business of selling, so you need to acquaint yourself
with at least the basics of successful sales techniques. Nevertheless,
it may suit you to have a business where the product or service
brings you repeat customers. There's a big difference in running a
business where your product gets consumed every day or every
week and running a business offering a product that's purchased
once every few years. And, of course, it will probably be easier to
persuade prospective customers to try your brand of pickles that
they've never heard of, and risk an outlay of £1.20, than to risk
£600 on your unfamiliar brand of sofa. But you would have to sell
a lot of jars of pickle to earn the same profit you'd make on a £600
sofa. Then again, if you were wholesaling your jars of pickles to
retailers or caterers you might sell £600-worth of pickles before
you'd sell one sofa.

That brings us to another choice when thinking about what sort of business you'd like to run: one dealing with consumers, i.e. the general public, or one that sells to other businesses. It's often said to be easier to start a small business where your customers are the general public, because there are greater opportunities for getting access to potential customers. Your product or service might be one for which every householder is a potential customer and therefore interested in your leaflet when it drops through their front door. Or every shopper at the local Saturday market could be a potential customer. Also, bear in mind that if your customers are other businesses you're likely to find that they expect time to pay for their purchases – they'll expect to be given 30 days' credit – even if it's for wholesale quantities of pickles.

In this first segment of your *Who am I?* questionnaire we've already flung out a number of possibilities for you to mull over including, we hope, some you haven't previously considered. It's good to have a choice and even better to know what those choices are.

2. What work do you have experience of?

If you've just left school or university your answer in this section is likely to be short. Or is it? We want you to include here any part-time jobs or temporary work you've had. Have you ever done any voluntary work or work-experience placements? Once you start to think about it, you may find you have more job experience than you realise. You'll see from the next couple of questions how some experience of different types of work or working environments could be useful to you in coming up with a business idea.

3. What skills did you acquire from the above work? And what knowledge?

4. What aspects of this work did you like?

5. (A) What qualifications (if any) do you hold?
    (B) What subjects have you studied?

6. (A) How do you spend your leisure time?
    (B) What else are you interested in?
    (C) When you go to the shops what sort of products do you look at?

In your answer to 6 (A), think about the skills and knowledge you've picked up through your leisure interests. For example, if you're good at football ask yourself why. What position do you play? Different positions require different skills and attributes.

Co-author Luke had always been interested in playing different sports, some of which required him to build on his fitness. This led to a general interest in getting and keeping fit and saw him spending many evenings and weekends at the gym. By the time he was looking for a business to start after leaving college, he'd learnt a lot about getting and staying fit. This prompted him to ask himself: 'Could I use that interest and knowledge to help others?' Luke took a course to obtain certification as a fitness instructor and at the age of 18 launched his own fitness instruction business. So what are you interested in that you do at evenings and weekends?

7. What else are you knowledgeable about?

Set down here the skills and knowledge you've acquired, firstly through good experiences, and secondly, not-so-good experiences.

8. **Any other skills?**

9. **What are your natural abilities?**
Write down here any abilities and talents that came easily to you.
For instance, are you talented at drawing?

A VALUABLE DOCUMENT

Your completed *Who Am I?* questionnaire will provide valuable
information for you to mine. It's worth making the effort and taking
time to give as much detail as you possibly can.

It's commonly assumed that to come up with a workable
business idea you need a sudden flash of inspiration. If you get
that sudden flash of inspiration, congratulations, but it's definitely
not essential. You can come up with a workable business idea by
another route.

What you need is something to start with. Something you can
work with. Something to set you off. Suppose, for example, your
answer to 6 (C) *When you go to the shops what sort of products
do you look at?* was clothes. That could give you a starting point
in your thinking. Perhaps 'clothes' might be a trade you could go
into? Once you've got a product to think about, you can then go
on to consider whether you'd like to retail this product line. Or
perhaps you could wholesale it. Or could you set up a business
that manufactures it? Imports it? Now you have a starting point in
your thinking, you've got lots to think about.

The answers to your *Who Am I?* questionnaire can give you
that valuable starting point you need for your thinking.

Phoebe liked baking cakes. She was so good that from time to time friends would ask her to make a cake for them for a special occasion such as a retirement do or even a wedding. When she was looking for a small business to start it seemed natural for her to do something she was good at and liked doing. For the most part she used recipes from old cookbooks and so her cakes were unlike the mass-produced products found in the supermarkets. They were different and more tasty. Phoebe found that because customers couldn't buy them in their local supermarket, they were prepared to purchase them by mail order. Safely packaged, of course.

This case study is a simple illustration of one of the most valuable lessons we have learnt in helping people come up with an idea for starting a business. We can't overemphasise the importance of realising that the starting point in your search for a business idea can be something very ordinary – an everyday product perhaps, or a skill or knowledge you have and which many other people possess. Because this knowledge or interest or skill or experience is commonplace, the danger is that you will not value it, or not value it sufficiently, and therefore overlook it. And yet it could give you the starting point you need: something to work with. Once you have something to work with, you can use the techniques, tools and approaches in the following chapters to mould it in to a workable business idea. Hopefully, into something that distinguishes it from the competition, from what is already out there, so that you will have customers for your product or service.

Your *Who am I?* questionnaire can be so useful in your search for a business idea that it's worth enrolling the help of other people, both in completing it and then in using it. Almost certainly, no matter how much effort you put into the questionnaire, your answers will be incomplete. This is because we don't see ourselves as others see us. If you were to ask a friend or a member of your family or some other relative to spot the gaps in your answers, there would likely be matters you have overlooked. For instance, you might have overlooked some skill because it's a skill that comes naturally to you, yet someone who does not possess that skill would probably be impressed by it and not overlook it. And we all have gaps in our memory. If you have a mate who is a good enough mate to put in the effort to help you with the questionnaire, they might remind you about something that happened three years ago and that you've forgotten about.

And then when your *Who am I?* questionnaire is as complete as it can be, don't just exhaust yourself by scrutinising it for starting points. Maybe your mate or your mum will help you. This could work really well if you have someone to help you who is also interested in setting up their own business. So can you think of someone among your friends who has at some time considered chucking in their job and setting up their own business? Show them what you're doing with the *Who am I?* questionnaire and, in return for their helping you to come up with an idea, you could help them think of their own business idea. You might even hit upon something you both want to do and end up as business partners.

There are all kinds of exciting prospects and possibilities opening up.

CHAPTER 4
WHAT MAKES THE DIFFERENCE?

Barrie has 14 years' experience as a trainer on business start-up courses and has worked with some 10,000 would-be entrepreneurs. At the end of these courses, some of those people, having learnt what was involved in setting up and running their own business, decided that it wasn't, after all, what they wanted to do. A few, as you might expect, set up a business which didn't work out for them. Others, far greater in number, set up a business that achieved what they wanted. And a percentage of those people set up a new enterprise that was outstandingly successful. Of course, that doesn't necessarily mean it brought those highly successful people great wealth: a business is successful if it achieves what you wanted it to achieve, which could be any of the objectives we looked at in Chapter 1.

What makes the difference? Why do some people manage to set up a business that is outstandingly successful?

If you take advantage of the business counselling that's available to you – often without charge – from organisations such as Business Link, local enterprise agencies and other organisations, you'll receive advice on a range of matters and we'll consider these in later chapters. This advice will include the need to look at the existing competition, to see whether there is a market for your product or service, the need for sufficient finance to set you up and keep you going for a while, and a variety of other fundamental issues that are vital and relevant. But there is one matter which may not appear on the business counsellor's list and yet, in our experience, perhaps deserves to top the list. How to explain this essential requirement? The following case study may help.

CASE STUDY

We were presenting our business start-up course in an affluent city in the South East. One of the participants stood out from the other young people owing to his strong northern accent. For the purposes of this case study we will call him Tony.

He told us that he didn't live locally and that he had travelled down from a small town in the North West. He'd read about the course in a national newspaper and made enquiries to see if it was to be held in his area. It wasn't, so he decided that if the course wasn't coming to him then he would come to the course. We were impressed by his motivation and initiative,

CASE STUDY

especially when he explained that he'd not been able to afford the fare to travel to where we were holding the course so he'd thumbed a lift. 'I'm getting desperate,' he added. 'I left school three years ago at 16 and I've never been able to get a job. There's a lot of unemployment where I live and I don't have any paper qualifications.'

By the end of the course, Tony was buzzing. He came to us and asked for feedback on two ideas – among the many he'd come up with using the techniques and approaches we suggest in this book. Our reaction to one of the ideas was that it was OK, and worth investigating, since we had previously helped someone with a similar idea. That person, like Tony, had needed to start a business on a shoestring and it had to be one which would produce income quickly. We were more enthusiastic about the second idea, since it seemed very much to suit his interests and the needs of the locality where he lived. Energised and enthusiastic, Tony returned home to set the wheels in motion, promising to keep in touch and let us know of his progress.

We were surprised when he didn't contact us and, when Barrie rang and spoke to him on the phone, Tony sounded a different person. He was dispirited and demoralised. He told Barrie that when he got home his dad had asked him if he'd come up with any ideas. When he revealed to his dad the idea we'd enthused over, Tony said his dad had screwed up his face and told Tony: 'If it's such a good idea, then why hasn't someone done it before?'

Tony ended his conversation with Barrie by saying: 'He's always like that my dad. He pours cold water on everything.'

We never heard from Tony again and doubt that he ever did set up in business. Yet from what we'd learnt about him over the duration of the course, it seemed to us that he had a lot going for him and that with the right idea he could have set up a successful small business. If it hadn't been for the major impediment he had to overcome: namely that he had someone in his life, affecting him, who had a negative attitude.
Is there someone like that in your life?

So, top of our list of attributes that will help you create and build a successful business is the right attitude. Having a positive attitude is probably the greatest asset you can have if you are setting up a business.

We can all feel downbeat or uncooperative or ill-tempered or demoralised at some point during the day. Perhaps your poor frame of mind was triggered by a road-rage incident; or you've had a letter from the bank this morning threatening to cut up your debit card; or a shop assistant who wouldn't believe you were over 18 was rude to you. But after a while your state of mind improves as the memory fades. Unfortunately, with some people, a poor frame of mind is not a temporary state; it is their usual state of mind.

What are the characteristics of a positive thinker? Watching and studying people who have set up and grown a successful business, we've seen the following factors at work.

■ **Perseverance.** If at first you don't succeed, try, try and try again. Don't say 'I can't find a decent supplier' and give up after contacting just three possible suppliers; you may have to contact three hundred.

- **TSD.** This stands for Try Something Different. If the conventional route hasn't worked, or what worked for others hasn't been successful for you, then you may have to try something unconventional. Something your mother wouldn't approve of!

- **Do It Now!** Why put it off if there's no good reason to do so and you could do it today?

- **Optimism.** It's 4.30 p.m. and you've been out all day making sales calls without signing up a customer. 'I'm having a bad day – no-one is going to give me an order so I might as well go home.' Wrong attitude. Instead, say to yourself: 'The next call might bring me the breakthrough.' It could be that the very last call of the day is the one where the customer is pleased to see you because you have got just what they need. Life is like that.

- **Positive thinkers feel good.** They feel good about themselves, about what they are doing and, later in life when they look back, they feel good about what they have achieved.

Make a conscious effort to develop an attitude of mind that uses the characteristics we've set out here. Our list of further reading in Appendix 3 includes a book on the subject of attitude and we recommend you read this. The right mental attitude could energise you and make you more productive. Negative thinking inhibits creativity and therefore impedes your ability to achieve. The right attitude will improve your relationship with others, including customers.

And a positive mental attitude improves your ability to make decisions. Such as the decision to set up your own business. It will also help you decide what your business idea will be and later help you to make decisions about suppliers, marketing campaigns, distinguishing yourself from the competition and even how to organise your office.

So hold a mirror up to yourself and ask: 'What is my attitude to the world?'

But also ask yourself: is there someone in your life – perhaps a member of your family, a neighbour or your so-called best mate – whose opinion of your starting a business would demotivate you and drain you of your energy and ambition? If so, you need to identify this person and deal with them. Probably the easiest way to deal with them is simply not to tell them your plans.

HOW TO GENERATE MORE IDEAS

A business starts with a business idea, so if we can enhance your ability to come up with ideas, that will be a major help. Bear in mind that, once you've come up with the idea for your business, that's just the start of your need for ideas. You'll have to come up with ideas for raising money, ideas for letting people know your business has been born, ideas for standing out from the existing competition, and on and on. And then when the business is up and running you'll need a constant stream of further ideas – for improving your service or product, for reducing costs or for making the business run more efficiently, and so on.

It's possible to argue that, barring accidents, everything that's achieved in life begins with an idea. So if you improve your ability to come up with ideas, you improve your ability to do just about anything. The good news is that your ability to generate ideas can quickly be improved by practice, by knowing and applying some useful techniques, and by working in a supportive environment. You can help create a supportive environment by not working with, or even talking to, people with a poor attitude.

G.I.G.

'Brainstorming' describes a session where a group of people come together for the sole purpose of generating ideas. Today it's often referred to as Group Ideas Generation, or G.I.G. for short.

Earlier we raised the possibility of your getting a friend or relative to help you come up with an idea by working with you on your *Who am I?* questionnaire. If you could persuade just two other people to help you, you'd have enough for an effective and productive team devoted solely to coming up with ideas. Can you think of any friends who have ever expressed an interest in setting up their own business? If so, give them a ring now and sound them out. Yes, do it now – remember the characteristics of the positive thinker! If you're a student, there are bound to be other students who are interested in setting up their own business, especially if you're a business studies student.

G.I.G. sessions can work really well. It may be that a suggestion from someone else stimulates your thinking, taking you along lines of thought you might not otherwise have gone down. Or one person might suggest something and someone else adds to it, then you add something more and, together, the group has created an idea that you may not have thought of on your own.

For G.I.G. sessions to be effective, certain rules have to be obeyed. Most important of these is that negative comments are banned. If someone comes up with an idea that you feel won't work, it's better to say nothing. This is because you need to build up momentum – you want members of the group to come up with as many suggestions as possible. If you demoralise a member of your group by criticising them in front of the others, they are likely to withdraw into their shell and not contribute. That would be a pity. Just because they came up with one poor idea doesn't mean they are incapable of coming up with valid suggestions later.

And there must be no evaluation during the session. This is the most difficult rule to enforce. If your friend comes up with an idea for a new business, the most natural reaction is for you to evaluate it, to say why you feel this is a workable idea or why you feel it isn't. But this slows down the momentum and, once again, you risk deflating a member of the group and inhibiting them through critical comments. Save the evaluation for later. This is such a vital rule, we repeat it: NO EVALUATION DURING G.I.G. SESSIONS. You can evaluate until your heart's content later.

DEADLINES

When you're young you might be tempted to think you've got plenty of time to come up with an idea and set up a business. That could be an impediment to coming up with a workable idea, as it could slow down your thinking. To come up with good ideas you need momentum. Indeed, the trick is to think of as many ideas as possible. If you come up with only three ideas, the chances of one of those being what you are looking for are slim. Come up with 30 ideas and you have a reasonable chance that one of them is what you need. Come up with 300 and there might be a golden nugget of an idea in there.

So set yourself a deadline. Give yourself a time limit for coming up with an idea that could make a workable business. However, be realistic with this time limit – don't let your enthusiasm run away with you and cause you to set a time limit of, say, tomorrow evening.

Setting a time limit is also a useful technique when it comes to actually starting a business. Let's say you've got your idea, you have fixed upon what it is you are going to do. But…you can't launch the business yet because you're about to go on holiday. Or you've got to decorate your flat. Or you want to use the money to change your car or… It's easy to find a reason to put off the actual launch date. If you think you're guilty of this, set yourself a time limit. And to prevent you from simply ignoring that looming date, announce it to the world. Tell everyone the date when you'll be setting up in business.

In particular, make sure you tell Mr or Ms Negative, who's convinced that you won't do it. Then as that date circled on the calendar gets closer you will have a real incentive to get on with it. Rather than see the old moaner proved right.

PRETEND YOU ARE SOMEONE ELSE

Sometimes coming up with ideas can be a bit of a laugh. Perhaps you've been sitting at the table trying to come up with an idea for half an hour and now you're stuck. Or you've been doing it with a friend or with a couple of mates in a G.I.G. session and you're *all* stuck. Perhaps the G.I.G. session started at 7 o'clock and it's now half past 11 and you've all run out of steam. So liven things up by pretending each of you is somebody else.

This somebody else could be a famous personality or it could be an inspired teacher from school or college or uni or someone you know who runs a successful business, or anybody from the past or present who is witty or a quick thinker. Better still, if that person is an original thinker, someone who doesn't think like most other people. For a few minutes pretend you are this person and try to think like them: what ideas would they come up with? Could you for a few minutes think like Sir Alan Sugar, founder of Amstrad, or Del Boy of the much-loved sitcom *Only Fools and Horses*?

ROAD BLOCKS

Your thinking can be blocked in, constricted, by impediments of which you may not be aware until we point them out.

Worrying about what other people will think can be one such impediment to your creativity. 'If I set up a business doing that, what will my dad think?' That might or might not be a legitimate concern. If your dad has valid points to make, then his input is something to consider; if he's worried that the neighbours will think you are stupid because all your mates have gone to university and you didn't want to, that's something else. Beware of other people wanting you to conform.

Another constriction on thinking is the fear of making yourself look an idiot in front of other people. If you tell a joke in front of your mates, you want them to laugh, but of course it's not the same if you unintentionally make a fool of yourself so that they laugh *at* you. So you might be in a G.I.G. session with a couple of your mates and you come up with an idea. You're about to give voice to it when you think to yourself: no – they'll think that's a stupid idea, they'll laugh at me. So you stay silent. Wrong.

The world wants to hear your silly-sounding ideas, because silly-sounding ideas can work in the real world. Someone in the past must have come up with the idea: 'What about turning up at a birthday party or leaving do dressed in a daft costume and singing a silly song? Do you think we can make a business out of that?' It's a good job somebody had the courage to make that suggestion or we wouldn't have profitable kiss-o-gram services. And there a number of successful mail-order catalogues and websites devoted to zany products that nobody needs but that, once someone's invented them, other people desire to own.

Reflecting on his *Who Am I?* questionnaire Nick, aged 24, had been a salesperson for the last six years, having worked for companies in three different industries. All his sales experience was confined to selling direct to consumers in the home rather than selling to businesses and Nick felt he had built up considerable expertise in this specialised field. So when he was looking for an idea for a business to start it struck him that a fairly comfortable way into business would be for him to set up doing something in an area he had lots of experience of. So he set up as a sales trainer, teaching other new or young sales trainees the techniques that he'd refined and that had worked for him.

'But it was never my intention to do that for a long time,' said Nick. 'I wanted to see if I liked running my own business and I also wanted to gain some confidence. I thought that setting up my own business was enough of a challenge in itself without my trying to climb Mount Everest, for instance by trying to get off the ground a new product that I'd devised and which nobody knew whether it was worth having. But every

sales organisation could see the benefit of sales training for
their new salespeople.'

After about 18 months, the business had taken off so Nick
felt confident enough to have a go at something more
challenging and set up a new business in the electronics
industry. This required a much bigger financial investment than
he'd needed for setting up his one-person training service and
he had to take on staff and deal with new challenges that he
would have perhaps found too overwhelming if this had been
his first business.

Is that an approach you could consider? Is it possible that you are
reading this book because you intend to set up *two* businesses –
one in the immediate future that would not be too challenging and
another at a later date, as a replacement, when you've gained
confidence and skills? If this thought hadn't occurred to you, then
perhaps you should think again…?

CHAPTER 5
THE PROVEN ROUTE TO A BUSINESS IDEA

Let's start your search for a business idea with some tried and tested approaches.

These routes to coming up with a viable business idea may not be ones that set your pulse racing with excitement, but they have been used successfully by many people and could work for you.

WHAT CAN'T YOU BUY?

One well-tried route to finding a gap in the market is to ask yourself this simple question: what's not available? Can you think of something a customer might want to buy but wouldn't be able to obtain?

Start with your own experience. Can you recall a product or service you've wanted in the past but weren't able to obtain? Perhaps it was something you couldn't buy locally or for which you couldn't find a supplier at all. Realistically, the older you are the more likely it is that this has happened to you, so ask relatives, friends and neighbours to trawl through their memories to think of something that they wanted to buy in the past and couldn't get hold of. Another possibility is that it could be something connected to the workplace – a product or service that was needed for the business or organisation and that couldn't be tracked down.

Don't confine your thinking to products or services that were impossible to get hold off. What about those items where you or other people had to settle for second best? In other words, you didn't get exactly what you were looking for but you did get something in the end.

And broaden your thinking to take into account products or services that you or other people wanted which were difficult but not impossible to get. Maybe there was an unacceptable wait before the product could be delivered or you or perhaps you had to travel to get it?

Extend your thoughts, too, to things that might be nice to have but that you haven't seen or been offered.

Gemma, like many people, was very fond of chocolate. She told us that in her search for a business idea she had been thinking about products she couldn't buy, that weren't available. She had a particular liking for continental chocolates, which are quite different in appearance and taste from traditional English chocolates. So she started to think that the chocolates and sweets that came from other countries further afield might also be different from the English product.

Gemma tracked down US suppliers of chocolates and other candy, as the Americans call their sweets, which were sufficiently different from what was available in the UK market. She began importing the chocolates and other candy and wholesaling them, but in the first few months she struggled to get retailers to accept the products. This was because it's often difficult at first to get people to accept something new, especially in the case of retailers as they naturally have doubts about whether something that the buying public has not seen before will sell. Gemma's breakthrough came when she managed to get the products into a number of department stores and delicatessens who were on the lookout for something different to offer their clients, something that was not available in the supermarkets.

AREA COMPARISON

Thanks to the Internet, today we have ready access to customers beyond our shores, but perhaps the business you set up will be one that serves your local community. Some products and services are unlikely to be provided by businesses from afar. Very few customers are likely to engage the services of a painter and decorator based a hundred miles away to redecorate their living room. And if you have a sudden yearn for some freshly baked fancy bread, you're going to shop locally for it. Also, many customers, particularly older customers, prefer to deal with a local supplier, especially if it involves inviting the supplier into their home. Indeed, as a small business, you can compete against national suppliers operating throughout the UK, including in your area, because you have the distinction of being a local business. This is an example of how in the right trade a small business can have an advantage over a major national corporation.

So in what field of activity could you set up as the local supplier? One proven way of spotting a gap in the local market is to compare like with like. If you live in a town or city or in a rural area where you have ready access to a centre of population, here is one approach you could take. Think about the character of the town or city and the different aspects of life in that town or city. For example, what sort of industries are found there? Does it have a tourist trade? Or a lot of high-tech industries? Or a number of manufacturers? Does it have a big university that attracts large numbers of students? It's important to consider who lives in the area – for instance, in a coastal area there may be a high proportion of retired people. Next, consider the geographical factors, such as whether your centre of population is located at the coast. These social, economic and geographic factors affect the type of businesses found – or which could be set up – in an area. So if you have tourists visiting your town, there will be businesses that cater for those tourists.

Having built up a picture of your area, now try to bring to mind another town or city that has a similar profile, a town or city that shares one or more of the major characteristics of your area. So, for example, if you live in Cambridge, it may strike you that Bath, like Cambridge, is a tourist area. Now ask yourself what businesses succeed in this other area. The thinking here is that if you can spot a business that is operating successfully in an area that in some way is similar to your own, you could perhaps set up the same type of business in your own area. So a resident of Cambridge might spot a business catering for the tourist trade in Bath and find there is no similar business in Cambridge. Or it may be that it's the type of business where there are a number of successful suppliers in this other area but not so many suppliers in your own area, which would indicate that there could be room in the marketplace for you.

CASE STUDY

Co-author Barrie was looking for a business to start after he had been made redundant. As he cast his mind back over the years trying to remember something that had at some time been difficult for him to buy, his wife reminded him of the occasion when they wanted to buy some made-to-measure furniture covers for their lounge suite. No such supplier of this product was to be found in the local Yellow Pages and Barrie and his wife had to contact a maker in the next county. This supplier was at first reluctant to travel the necessary distance to give them a quote for new covers for their suite.

So when Barrie was looking for a business to start he set up as the local supplier of made-to-measure loose furniture covers, thereby meeting a gap in the local market. As he had no local competition, the business took off from week one, gradually expanded and was operated by Barrie for some three years before being sold as a going concern.

You don't have to rely solely on your existing knowledge of other areas; you can easily find out from the Internet or Yellow Pages what's available elsewhere and which businesses are doing well.

Many libraries, including some university and college libraries, carry Yellow Pages for the entire UK.

Adam was a business studies student attending university in a historic city that attracted tourists from both within the UK and overseas. The city's attraction as a tourist venue was partly due to its strong association with the Romans, with Roman archaeological remains for tourists to visit.

Adam was struck by the numbers of tourists, especially from overseas, piling into an American-style ice-cream parlour. He figured that if overseas tourists had a taste for varied and novel American-inspired ices in his university city, then such a business might work elsewhere. When he finished his studies at uni he produced a shortlist of three cities which attracted large numbers of overseas tourists. In the second on his list he was able to track down suitable and affordable premises to open his American-style ice-cream parlour. It was so successful that within a year he was able to open a second parlour in another city with a similar profile.

WHAT'S ABROAD?

It's likely that at some time you've enjoyed an overseas holiday, either with your family or with your mates. Perhaps you've even taken a year out and been back-packing around the world. Thinking about the good times you had could give you the starting point you're looking for in your search for a business idea. Can you recall some product you saw overseas or some service that's not available in the UK? Could you import that product or could you set up a similar service here?

Kelly was on holiday with her boyfriend in Scandinavia. Visiting small local shops off the tourist track she came across a retailer with a range of children's wooden toys. The designs were unlike those she had seen in the UK and were so attractive and full of play value that she immediately turned to her boyfriend and said: 'That's what I'm going to do. I shall go home and set up as a supplier of wooden toys like this.'

Kelly didn't import the toys, but brought home a range of samples and then, taking inspiration from, but not copying them, she devised her own range. These she had made for her under contract with a small manufacturer in the UK and the timber used was from sustainable sources grown specifically for commercial use. Kelly cashed in on the growing interest in children's products that don't harm the environment.

Research can be fun. How about finding out what exporters overseas have to offer? You can spend many enjoyable hours leafing through catalogues and looking up websites that will offer you a dazzling array of products available around the world.

Many countries have trade organisations which actively promote their products for export. This, as you might expect, is especially true of some Asian countries whose economies have in recent years undergone massive expansion and development. China is the most obvious example and others include Vietnam, Korea, Taiwan and Thailand. If you contact the trade promotion body for any of these countries you'll be put in touch with suppliers of products in which you are interested. To find the name of the appropriate trade promotion organisation, type into a search engine relevant words such as 'overseas trade promotion' and then the name of the country. Very likely the website for the principal trade promotion body for a given country will invite you to submit details of your interests. They will then pass on your contact details to manufacturers and exporters in their country, who in turn will contact you direct.

Some of the countries with the biggest export trades will offer you the opportunity to subscribe to periodic listings. These publications will regularly provide details of the latest offerings from manufacturers of a particular type of product. For example, you may find that for a very modest outlay you can subscribe to a periodic listing of all the latest offerings from jewellery manufacturers within that particular country. This could be a way for you to have a constant source of supply of new products to offer your customers.

So are there any complications involved in importing products? You can get a lot of useful information from Business Link (**www.businesslink.gov.uk**). Duty (tax) may have to be paid on imports of the products you have in mind, although this could be a comparatively small sum. And there will be paperwork to complete. But if you are first in the market with a new product or you are able to offer something different from what most of the existing competition is offering, the effort involved in importing it might prove extremely beneficial for you.

THE PENDULUM FACTOR

When you've come up with an idea for a product or service that's not available, ask yourself: why isn't it available for people to buy? The answer may be that nobody wants it. Or it's not widely available because there's only a tiny demand for it. The fact that there's only a very small demand for a product or service could work in your favour. Maybe you're intending to set up a business that grows to be a worldwide multinational corporation or are your ambitions more limited? Perhaps you need only a part-time business activity to help support you while you are studying, for example? Or do you plan to be the proud proprietor of a small business that employs only you, or one that grows to employ only a dozen others? Bear in mind that a small business can survive in small markets, whereas big business needs big markets. This is good news if you plan to run a small business, as it means you can make a business out of a market that big corporations will pass by.

Many new businesses take off because they launch into a growing market, supplying a product or service for which there is an increasing demand. This means there's room in the marketplace for a new business even though there may be lots of competitors. With more new customers coming into the market every day, some of those new customers can come to this new business. But there can also be opportunities for new businesses in declining markets, with products or services for which there are fewer buyers than previously. Don't automatically dismiss going into a field where the market is shrinking. Remember, big business needs big markets and big companies need lots of customers, but your small business doesn't. So if you can spot a trade or industry which is declining, and where the big players in the field are getting out, then it could be time for you to consider moving in.

There's an interesting phenomenon known as the pendulum factor. Sometimes a new product is launched on the market and has such a widespread impact that it appears that it has entirely superseded that which has gone before. An example is the home computer, or PC. You are probably unlikely to remember a time when your parents sat at a word processor or, before that, a typewriter. Those functions have of course been incorporated into the PC and there was a time some years ago when nobody would consider purchasing a typewriter or word processor. They were finished, unsaleable, confined to car-boot sales. But in the last couple of years word processors have reappeared in some catalogues, where the blurb tells us they are ideal for people who are looking only to type simple documents and who don't want the complexities of a computer and all the things it can do – including breaking down.

And – astonishingly – in some catalogues a product has recently reappeared that many people thought had become a museum piece: the manual typewriter – the predecessor of the electric typewriter, which was itself the predecessor of the word processor. Who on earth would buy a manual typewriter? A friend tells us that his aunt has recently bought one. Why? Why buy something that has a limited function and is slow and laborious to use. 'Because it's a mechanical product and of comparatively simple construction, so there is almost nothing to go wrong. And my aunt loves the sound it makes, the click-click-click of a manual typewriter.' Click, click, click? What that product seems to have is a degree of charm that the modern computer lacks.

This is an example of the pendulum factor at work. Along comes a product which sweeps away its predecessors – nobody buys that old thing any more! Then, when the dust has settled, after a few years some buyers emerge and they want what has gone before and it starts to reappear on the market in very small quantities. But there may be enough buyers to make a market for a very small business.

And don't overlook products that simply go out of fashion – and then come back again. Can you recall something you've used or played with in the past, perhaps a craze line that now could be resurrected and introduced to a market of younger buyers – younger even than you – who have not seen it before?

New products can be exciting – but making a successful business out of old products can also be exciting.

CHAPTER 6
I'VE NOT SEEN THAT BEFORE

Let's look at the possibility that your new business could take the form of a brand-new product that you devise yourself and launch on to the world.

Now, at that suggestion, you might be tempted to skip this chapter. It's possible your reaction is: 'I'm not an inventor! I couldn't invent something new.'

The good news is that you don't have to be an 'inventor' to come up with a new product. You don't need to be a boffin or an electronics whiz kid or a computer genius. Once you start to look closely at new products launched on the marketplace you'll find that the overwhelming majority of them are not the products of mad inventors. Most new products are not totally unlike anything else that's gone before. It's true that a tiny minority are completely revolutionary and take the world by storm, but you could take an alternative approach that many other people and businesses commonly take. The easiest route to creating a new product is to take an existing product and modify it – take what is there now and change it.

Your reaction to that suggestion is likely to be: 'To what extent do I have to modify what is there now?' The answer is that you must modify the existing product to the extent that it strikes potential customers as new. Your task is to invoke in prospective buyers the reaction: 'I haven't seen that before.' If it's new to them, then you have pulled it off – you can claim to be launching a new product on to the world.

Having corrected the misconception that you have to be either a brilliant inventor or a corporation with millions of pounds to spend on research and development in order to be able to devise and launch a new product, you may still have other doubts. Doubt about money is probably one of them. Surely a new product would involve you in huge development costs for matters such as research and prototypes and tooling up? Possibly, but not necessarily. It depends on the type of product you are devising. Many products lend themselves to simple manufacturing processes. It could be something that you can work on at home to begin with, such as an item of clothing. And plenty of people have put together some gadget or device in their garage. You can take inspiration from what others have done without having a fat bank balance.

On the other hand, if you come up with an idea which requires capital sums beyond your reach, there are other possibilities. Do not immediately discard these ideas as unworkable. One possibility is for you to approach an established manufacturer and agree with them that they will do the costly development, market research and promotional work, in return for paying you a licence fee, which could be a percentage of their return. Or, if that doesn't appeal to you, put your brilliant idea on the back-burner and come up with another idea that you can work on in the meantime. This second, more accessible idea that you can get off the ground in no time could then be a source of finance for your original idea. Plough a percentage of your profits from that into working on your big idea.

As with other routes to coming up with a business idea, you need some starting points in your thinking. As we go through these, remember that your task is to invoke in prospective customers the response: 'I haven't seen that before – that's different.'

THE BEST ONE IN THE WORLD

Could you take some product that you're familiar with or which interests you and come up with a version that is simply the best one in the world? After all, if yours really is the best, then surely you'll be able to find customers for it on the basis that there are always people out there who want the best. You can also usefully apply this line of thinking to services: perhaps your product could take the form of a service which is simply the best of its type.

If you describe your product as being the 'best', this claim could rest on a number of factors. Perhaps your product is the best because similar products are known to be unreliable and yours is ultra-reliable. Or maybe you have the best back-up service. Or your claim could be based upon your product being the most luxurious version. If we asked you what is the best car in the world, you might respond: 'The Rolls-Royce'. What do we associate with a Rolls-Royce? We associate it with high-quality engineering, reliability – and luxury. Nobody *needs* luxury, but some people desire it and some of those people can afford to pay for it. So could you come up with a product or a service that is the most luxurious of its kind?

Of course, your luxury version would likely be the most expensive one on offer, which in turn means it would probably have only a small market. But that's OK, as we've seen that a small business can exist in a small market. Your reaction may also be that the costliest version will suffer unduly in those periodic recessions that free-enterprise economies suffer from time to time. Quite likely, but people with the deepest pockets usually don't suffer as much as the rest of us ordinary mortals and even in the worst economic times seem to have enough money for life's luxuries. Also, bear in mind that the rest of us are often prepared to splash out on special occasions, even in hard times.

CASE STUDY

Shortly after graduating, Mark's best mate from uni invited him and others from their student days to his wedding. He was marrying the daughter of a wealthy ex-banker and it was a grand do. The reception took place in an enormous marquee set up on the immaculate front paddock of the family's imposing Queen Anne property. Mark was hugely impressed with the catering, the quartet, the dazzling display of gifts. But he found himself stepping out of this sumptuous world when he needed to go round the back of the marquee to the portable toilets. These didn't seem so very different from the portable loos at the music festivals he and his mates had been to in their student days. He had to negotiate the rickety steps up into cabins where water or some other fluid swilled around the floor, to be greeted by an aroma that was nothing like that given out by the array of fresh flowers in the marquee. Mark's reaction was: 'What a spoiler!'

Over a six-course meal he and his former fellow student, Darren, agreed that while the food and the wine were outstanding, under their noses was a service crying out to be improved.

Mark and Darren's Grand Portable Loos come with a uniformed attendant, real oil paintings in gilt frames, luxurious deep-pile carpeting and a welcome aroma. The cost raises the eyebrows of some prospective customers but Mark's reaction is: 'Why spoil a grand occasion for the sake of just a few hundred quid?'

PRODUCT COMBINATION

This is one of the simplest and yet most effective techniques for invoking that 'I've not seen that before!' response in prospective customers.

Take an existing product, something with which prospective customers are already familiar, then search the world for a second existing product, and bring the two together. Your business will be a dating agency for products, bringing together two items in a happy combination. It's the element of combination that strikes prospective customers as new. They have seen the individual items before but they haven't seen them married up.

At the age of 24 Samantha found herself single again after going through a separation. She felt it was a good time for a new beginning in her life. Samantha also yearned for financial independence, so she wanted to set up a new business.

Like most of us, she enjoyed her food but in her *Who am I?* questionnaire she also put cooking at the top of her list of interests. She decided to set up a food business, but her first product was not something she had made herself.

Honey is a good steady seller and with today's increasing interest in organic foods Samantha decided to source a supplier of organic honey. But how would she distinguish this from what the existing competition offered? An hour spent on the Internet uncovered an importer of soft toys whose new range included an appealing furry teddy bear no taller than the average honey jar. Samantha put this appealing little bear in a golden cardboard box along with a jar of honey. Customers hadn't seen this before: the little bear who just longed to be taken home together with his jar of organic honey, in his attractive gift box. This was Samantha's first new product.

What Samantha did in the early days of her business can give any new entrepreneur food for thought. Using the product combination technique proved to be a winner for her, but note that the teddy and his honey were presented in a gift box. Samantha did not always do the obvious. When most people set up as a manufacturer or wholesaler of foodstuffs their initial reaction is to try and get the product into the supermarkets. Today some supermarkets do have a policy of purchasing a percentage of their stock from regional suppliers, but it's still a very big mountain for a new business to climb. The company's buyer is likely to ask: 'Where is your track record?' The next question could be: 'Will you be able to meet demand if this product takes off?' And then there are stringent quality requirements, possibly demands for exclusivity, and credit stipulations that may all be too much of a headache for the fledging business.

Samantha felt it would be easier to deal with small, independent businesses at first and there were thousands of examples of those in the retail gift trade. So, rather than try and knock on the door of the big supermarket chains, she decided to concentrate on getting her product into some of the thousands of gift shops found in tourist areas and at stately homes, wildlife parks and historic cathedrals. She was offering a new product for the customer in the gift shop who was looking for something to take back home as a small gift for uncle and auntie, their attention caught by that appealing little bear and his honey, sitting on the shelf. Even if the lucky recipient of this gift didn't like the bear, they could always put the honey on their toast.

So what two things can you marry up to create your new product?

SOMETHING THAT NO LONGER EXISTS

This new product of yours needn't be something you've created, something that never existed before. It could be a product which used to be available but can't be bought today – an item from times past that you could reproduce. This is another way of inducing that all-important response: 'I haven't seen this before'. If prospective customers haven't seen it before, they'll regard it as something new. It might be something that can still be used today, or more likely, something ornamental.

One of the authors is a regular viewer of the popular BBC1 television series *Antiques Roadshow*. He doesn't have to watch more than two or three episodes of the show before he spots something that someone has found in the attic for which there could be a market today.

Where else to find inspiration? Why not try the local museum? Libraries and bookshops can also be a goldmine for prospectors of products to reproduce. Leaf through books on collectable items, on crafts and especially books featuring old recipes. Even better are old recipe books themselves. You might pick up a 19th-century book featuring recipes from the local area in a backstreet second-hand bookshop. Again, take inspiration from what others before you have done: many successful small businesses have been established in the food trade by providing an alternative to the mass-produced standard product. Without the benefit of mass production, and with the increased cost of unusual ingredients, your product would most likely retail at a much higher price than its mass-market counterpart, but if people come across something they really like to eat, that they find especially tasty, they will often find the extra few pounds to pay for it, perhaps as a small treat for themselves.

Leafing through a book of old regional recipes, Paul came across a recipe for a meat pie called Gamekeeper's Delight. Fed up with his job at the local council, which he'd had since leaving college, Paul had recently been wondering about the possibility of starting his own business. Food was a product that appealed to him and it's a classic example of the consumable product. If you come up with a food product that people like, they'll come back for it time and again.

With the aid of his girlfriend, Paul made up some sample Gamekeeper's Delight pies and took one down to a local pub that served bar meals. The recipe used game meats – a mix of rabbit, venison and hare – in a gravy made with sloes from the hedgerow. 'Very tasty but too upmarket for me', was the opinion of Paul's local publican. But he suggested that Paul try wine bars, which might be pleased to have the opportunity to offer their clients something different.

That saw the start of a business supplying to wine bars and gastropubs a range of pies and other products made from recipes found in old, ragged books hunted down in second-hand bookshops.

Reproducing items from bygone days can make a good business for supplying the gift trade. Think of all those times during the year when people are looking for a present for someone – birthdays, anniversaries, Mother's Day, Father's Day, weddings and, of course, Christmas. Buyers of gifts are often less concerned about the price than you might expect, enabling you to work on higher margins or to have a product that involves higher costs. Buyers are sometimes desperate to discover something suitable for the recipient and/or are looking for something different. If you've got that something different, they may be relieved and pleased – even though it costs more than they were planning to pay.

MAKE THEM SMILE

A big percentage of products bought as gifts are novelty products – something that you might not buy for yourself but which you'll buy as a gift in the hope that it will raise a smile on the face of the lucky recipient.

This market for novelty products provides another route for you to take and one with many possibilities. You might be able to spot some boring utilitarian product to which you could add appeal by giving it some novelty aspect. New examples of this are always coming on to the market and can be found on Internet websites and in mail-order catalogues specialising in gifts and unusual items. Many workplaces have a more relaxed atmosphere than previously and in the office you can spot more and more examples of novelty products. One of the authors has a solicitor friend – a senior partner in an upmarket firm of legal eagles – who has on his desk a stapler which takes the form of a plastic alligator with bulging eyes, whose jaws, instead of snapping off your fingers, will staple your papers. His daughter had bought it for him as a birthday present.

Every so often a unique, novelty version of a product appears on the market. Realistically, though, there are fewer product lines still waiting for somebody to produce the first novelty version. So it might be quicker and easier for you to take a product line for which there is an existing established market for novelty versions and come up with a new, additional novelty version.

Once you start thinking about and researching business opportunities and business ideas you never know where it might lead you! As an animal lover, Emma had decided while still at school that she wanted to make a career out of working with animals. She enrolled on an animal care course at her local college but at the end of the two years realised that working with animals was not the same thing as having your own pets. However, her interest in animals made her think that she could perhaps set up a business not actually working with animals but providing products for them. That could include training aids or toys for dogs.

Researching what products were available from exporters overseas took Emma on to the website for the Hong Kong Trade Development Council. This lead to her making contact with a manufacturer in China whose range incorporated not products for dogs but products which featured dogs. These included an umbrella whose wooden handle took the form of a spaniel's head, complete with moving eyes and drooping ears. A sample sent by airmail convinced Emma that this would make a product for gift buyers and it was so appealing that a dog-lover would also be tempted to buy it for themselves. This proved to be the first in a range of novelty umbrellas featuring the heads of different cartoon-like animals, including a duck, a donkey and a tortoise.

Emma's business illustrates an aspect of the gift trade that merits serious consideration. The overwhelming majority of buyers of her novelty umbrella are unlikely to have purchased it because they *needed* it. It's very likely that they already possessed a boring, functional umbrella. Most purchases of Emma's doggy umbrella will have been impulse purchases. The customer saw it, found it appealing and decided to have one. They now probably had two umbrellas. Indeed, since Emma over a period of time came to offer a range of her novelty brollies, she began to suspect that some people had bought more than one, adding to their collection as appealing new animal friends appeared in the store.

Coming up with an appealing novelty version of a product is a way to expand the market. Customers buy not because they need a product but because, having seen it, they desire it.

But of course they can't desire it until you have created it. This is an example of how creativity in business can generate new business opportunities, by expanding the market.

Get creative!

CHAPTER 7
A BUSINESS WITH A BIG HEART

How about setting up a business that makes you a profit – so you can pay the rent/mortgage, go to the supermarket, have a good night out – and which changes the world for the better?

We call this a business with a social aspect. It's one where the objective is to go beyond making a necessary profit and which meets some social need – something that benefits your local community or even perhaps the wider world.

It's possible of course to argue that any business which meets the needs and wants of customers at a price they can afford is of benefit to society. Well, almost any business.

Supplying guns to bank robbers can hardly be of social benefit.

There are many possibilities here. It could be that your business has an educational aspect to it, educating the public about something that is in their interest to know but which other businesses are perhaps not keen to reveal. So you might, for example, be supplying a food product and, with it, providing full details of how that foodstuff was produced, including details of your animal welfare standards. Or perhaps your business has a reformative aspect, where you are attempting to influence public opinion and change buying habits.

There are compelling reasons for you to consider setting up a business with a social aspect. In addition to benefiting the community it might have enormous benefits for you. Top of the list of your possible benefits is that you could attract customers who might not have come to you if you were running a conventional business. Indeed, it might be in their interests to be a customer of your enterprise rather than the competition. Let's suppose you were running a business that supplied a 'green' product. A company that is in need of green credentials, such as one in an industry which is perceived as being generally detrimental to the environment, might consider that by dealing with your business they will be seen to be enhancing their green credentials. The benefit you could provide to that company might outweigh considerations of price so that, even if your green product came with a higher price ticket than a competitor's, the company would still opt for your product or service.

As always, you need some starting points in your thinking.

A CAUSE CLOSE TO YOUR HEART

Is there some cause that you believe in and care about? Perhaps you have a particular concern for or interest in conservation and the protection of the environment? Or the welfare of children or the elderly? Or animal welfare? If so, thinking about these matters might lead you to a business idea. If, for example, you're interested in the environment, could there be a business opportunity in helping to alleviate noise pollution or protecting or preserving some resource? Combine your knowledge and interest in this cause with your knowledge of other matters, including other products. So, can you think of a product where you could enhance its green characteristics by reducing its packaging or using alternative ingredients? Go back to your *Who Am I?* questionnaire and see if something there sets you thinking.

On holiday in a part of the UK she had never visited before, Vanessa was surprised to find that the menu of the hotel she stayed in was heavily dependent on meat. As a longstanding vegetarian, she told the waiter she was repulsed by the thought of eating 'corpse and chips'. The offer to make her an omelette was met with a polite rejection accompanied by her pointing out that there were now a huge range of meat-free alternatives available. Meat-free burgers, sausages, substitutes for chicken nuggets, tasty bacon rasher look-a-likes: why weren't these alternatives on the menu? Was the proprietor not aware that there were now over three million vegetarians in the UK? And, of even more relevance to a business, research showed that more and more people were reducing their meat intake and looking for alternatives – especially younger people, and especially younger women, she added.

Vanessa discovered that her hotel's offering was not untypical in that part of the UK and that most hotels, guesthouses, restaurants and clubs still offered meat-heavy menus. There must be a market here, she concluded, for supplying wholesale a range of meat-free alternative products to catering establishments. A market did exist, but Vanessa found it was a tough one to crack and it took seven months of slog before her business regularly produced sufficient income for her to live on.

Vanessa is the first to admit that there must be markets where it's much easier to get a business off the ground. But she did create a business, a successful business, which at the same time as providing a profit had, in her eyes, additional benefits for both animals and people. For Vanessa passionately believes that what she is doing is in the interests of animal welfare, particularly in the light of the UK's reliance on imports of meat from countries with lower welfare standards than the UK. And she believes it's in the interests of people's health for them to at least reduce their intake of meat and that there is growing evidence of the connection between a high intake of meat and heart disease and various cancers.

Setting up and attempting to build a business with a social aspect gave Vanessa advantages that might be denied to the competition. Yes, her product in that particular market made for a challenging business start-up, but its proprietor had more energy than most budding entrepreneurs. Her motivation, her enthusiasm, her desire to make a success of the business was powered by her desire not just to make a profit but by her staunch belief that what she was doing was in the interests of both people and animals. Vanessa had a double dose of motivation, which helped make her more resilient, better able to withstand the bumps and obstacles and rejections she faced in getting her new business off the ground.

Over time she realised her business, with its social aspect, had another advantage – conviction. When a salesperson makes a presentation, we know they are trying to persuade us to make a purchase. Possibly this would involve us, the potential purchaser, in doing something we are reluctant to do or which we are unsure about committing ourselves to. We know that, in trying to convince us, the salesperson is showing their product in the best possible light. And that, in their enthusiasm to make a sale, they may even be tempted to overstate the benefits of the product.

But listen to Vanessa for a few minutes and you cannot help but be struck by her sincerity. Her belief in what she's trying to do, her belief in her product and her belief that, in a small way, she is trying to change the world for the better, all shines through. This is not just a salesperson trying to make another sale to get their commission.

It's a highly effective sales presentation. So what cause do you care about that would enable you to impress potential customers by the sincerity of your sales presentation?

WHAT MAKES YOU FROWN?

Another possible starting point in your thinking is to remind yourself of what you disapprove of. What is it that existing suppliers of products and services do, that you resent? And that, if you were a competitor, you would change? What would you do in a different way, so that you could stand out from the competition?

Today, we are accustomed to bodycare products being available in plain, simple packaging, if that's what we as customers choose to buy. However, there was a time, not so long ago, when it was the norm even for routine toiletries and cosmetics to come in elaborate packaging. Anita Roddick, founder of The Body Shop, the international chain of bodycare products, resented this. She felt that over-elaborate packaging of everyday products added unnecessarily to the cost and was a waste of the world's resources. So she set up a business where these products were available in plain, simple, comparatively low-cost, packaging.

So what winds you up?

SPREADING THE BENEFIT

The proprietor of a business needs that business to provide him or her with the benefit of a profit. But maybe you'd like to set up and run a business that also brought benefit to others involved in the business? This benefit would not take the form of a share of the profits, but some other advantage that the competition was not giving to them.

An example of this could be that your business brings benefit to its suppliers. In recent years, there's been a growing interest in Fairtrade products, so much so that supermarkets have caught on to this and now provide space on their shelves for Fairtrade items, especially popular foodstuffs such as coffee and bananas. Products with small markets are more likely to be found in small independent retailers, especially products where the sales volume is insufficient to justify floor space in a multiple high-street retail outlet.

In a society where people are better educated, they are more likely to want information about the products they purchase. This partly accounts for the growth in the popularity of Fairtrade products since, often, the more we learn about how a product is produced and distributed the more concerned we become. A big and growing percentage of concerned consumers want to know that what you are offering them is the result of a fair deal for those who made the product or contributed to its distribution. They want assurances that no damage is done to the producer's community and the environment. Such is the interest in Fairtrade products that you can now track down specialist wholesalers who supply a range of these products.

An obvious way to benefit customers is by helping those with limited incomes to make their money go further. Even in our comparatively affluent society many people, for a variety of reasons, have to exist on what other people would regard as too small an income. The group who have the smallest spending power may find themselves priced out of more affluent towns and cities.

In one small city we're familiar with, an above-average proportion of residents enjoy an above-average income. So, not surprisingly most of the local retail outlets cater for them. In addition, this city is a tourist area attracting many visitors from overseas, so other retail outlets cater for the tourists, who have spending money for the sort of things tourists buy. Neither the affluent bulk of the population nor the hundreds of thousands of tourists are likely to be purchasers of the cheapest goods, so there are no pound shops, no clearance outlets and no factory shops offering bargain-basement prices. Instead, low-income customers had to rely on the Sunday market on a council car park. When the council refused to renew the market operator's lease and the market closed, the howls of protest demonstrated the need for a source of bargain-price goods. Letters to the local newspapers were a reminder of how low-income buyers were very much overlooked by businesses.

Of course, there are well-established, multiple high-street retailers offering discount prices in certain lines, especially clothes and food lines. But the new small independent business may be able to compete against and even undercut these. There is an exciting trade world waiting to be discovered: the clearance industry. Throughout the year, huge quantities of all types of goods are sent to clearance warehouses to be sold off to traders at a fraction of their normal retail price. There are two main reasons why this happens. Some products are affected by changes in the season, the most obvious example being clothes. When spring comes, much of the winter lines, such as heavy clothing and darker colours, will be moved into clearance warehouses, to be followed in autumn by the summer lines in their bright colours and light fabrics. Another common source of clearance goods is catalogue stock: a change of catalogue means many of the lines previously offered will disappear from the new edition.

Old stock sitting in a warehouse involves costs: the money tied up in the stock itself plus warehousing overheads and insurance costs. Sometimes there may be higher stocks of clearance lines than usual, for instance, as a result of the weather. If there's a wet summer, sales of T-shirts and shorts in the shops will drop dramatically; a rise in their stocks at the clearance warehouse increases the need to get them moving. Hence, it's possible to locate sources of supply of clearance lines at 20 per cent, 10 per cent or even as low as 5 per cent of retail prices.

You can track down wholesale suppliers of clearance lines on the Internet, but when buying stock unseen it's important to read the description carefully. In particular, there's a big difference between brand-new stock which is sold as perfect and stock which has been out to customers and then returned. Customer returns might simply have occurred because the item was unsuitable and the retailer has a policy of accepting returns within a stipulated period. However, the item might have been returned because it was faulty. Even non-faulty returns may have their problems, such as the customer having repacked it badly or having forgotten to put all the parts back in the box. So expect a big trade price differential between perfect stock and customer returns. One of the best-known source for supplies of clearance lines is the monthly journal *The Trader*, which is on sale in some high-street newsagents, or if not, ask your friendly local newsagent to order the current copy for you.

Vicky needed to boost her income if she was to start her second year at college. A Saturday job in a local supermarket hadn't worked out: she'd had the misfortune to find herself with a section manager she didn't get on with and it had got to the stage where she almost dreaded going to work. And her earnings from the Saturday job weren't enough; she could also have worked two or three evenings at the supermarket but she hated the thought.

She liked the products that most 17-year-old females liked – clothes, cosmetics and jewellery in particular – but felt she never had enough money to buy all of these that she wanted.

One line she liked but didn't buy very often was hair accessories and she had noticed these were sold in the supermarket where she worked. Although many of the food lines sold in the supermarket were priced very competitively, the small stock of hair accessories struck her as expensive for what they were – but there were some nice items she would have liked. Was this something she could sell more cheaply than the supermarket?

One of her mates who also worked there was doing a business studies diploma. He told her that in the case of hair accessories and jewellery the supermarket worked on high margins because these were impromptu purchases, something the customer would see and treat themselves to while doing the food shopping. Her mate's dad knew something about clearance lines as he used to work for a mail-order catalogue and Vicky began to wonder if she couldn't set up her own little part-time business.

The first copy of *The Trader* she bought had three or four trade advertisements to which she replied but it turned out that none of them had what she was looking for. Vicky was disappointed but fortunately she didn't give up. The next month a different advertiser appeared promising some bargain price lines in jewellery and hair accessories. Vicky gambled £200 on a sample order and was thrilled to find most of the stock comprised lines from well-known high-street retailers since the stock bore the original barcode prices. Some of these jewellery lines retailed at up to £10 although the majority sold in the shops for between £3 and £5. The stock cost Vicky 25p per item. Emboldened by this

CASE STUDY

she went on to track down a supplier of clearance cosmetics and was able to offer her customers discontinued ranges of famous makes at as little as 20 per cent of the retail price they had sold for in the stores. Vicky made most of her sales through jewellery and cosmetic parties and within a couple of months was earning from her part-time business two to three times what she'd earned from her part-time job – without having to look out for that obnoxious manager.

Vicky says: 'Of course there are drawbacks to buying clearance lines and these have to be weighed against the low trade prices. Commonly you will have little or no choice about what goes in your particular lot.' So for example Vicky found that with the clearance jewellery one lot would contain mostly jewellery from one particular store, giving her a restricted range; in the next lot there might be almost no lines from that store. In the next delivery 50 per cent of the stock was bangles; the delivery after that it was nearly all rings and necklaces. And, unlike when purchasing standard stock items that can be re-ordered from a traditional wholesaler or importer, Vicky found that if a line took off and sold well she might never be able to get any more of the same.

On the other hand, Vicky lived in a city with large estates, where many of the inhabitants were on a low income. She says she particularly enjoyed holding parties in those localities where single mums, pensioners and teenage girls, among others, could go away clutching a handful of items they had been able to afford, each of which would give them some pleasure and which they'd purchased for comparatively little money.

THE PEOPLE YOU WORK WITH

Go out of your way to do something for the people you work with in your new business, and it could be your new business that benefits the most. Do something for people you take on to work with you, over and above what your competitors offer their staff, and you could find you have more customers than those competitors.

Jamie knew what it was like to be unemployed; he'd had five months of it. That was four years ago when he was 19, but he hadn't forgotten what it was like. He'd been made redundant at a time when unemployment was on the increase and he knew from the experience that in the part of the UK where he lived there were plenty of people unemployed who would make good employees.

A friend's uncle, now retired, formerly ran a mobile security business. Uniformed security staff, operating from vans, visited premises at random times while they were closed. Such a business had the advantage of lower costs in comparison to using static security officers who were present at the premises for long periods of time. But how to stand out from competitors offering a similar mobile security service?

Jamie decided that his firm would employ only people who had been unemployed for a period of three months or more. In addition to providing training in aspects of security work, he would allow each member of staff half a day off work each week on full pay to undertake training in other aspects of work, such as administration, secretarial duties and computing. These additional skills would make the staff more employable in the future.

These features, taking on unemployed people and training them, seemed to be all for the benefit of the staff, but in practice they boosted the attractiveness of the business to certain types of potential customers. Within two months of starting out, Jamie had signed up the local council. When choosing the contractor to provide security services, the local authority was attracted to a company that was helping to reduce the dole queue. By using the services of Jamie's company the council could be seen to be indirectly helping to reduce unemployment in the local community it served, since Jamie's business was a local business. This social aspect of Jamie's enterprise also appealed to other sectors of the market: a national charity with a regional headquarters located in Jamie's town was the next major client to sign up.

Changes in society throw up business opportunities and probably the biggest change facing us all today is climate change. Here, there must be endless opportunities for new enterprises, for young people with new ideas and a new approach to providing the green services and green products we will need. So many business opportunities that enable you to feel good about what you are doing.

As a teenager *Ed Miller* took a keen interest in conservation and was particularly concerned about the dwindling rainforest and its effect on the environment. That interest in conservation stayed with him and, when he was looking for a business to start, the question was: could he use that laudable interest to come up with a business idea?

We're all familiar with the plastic cups that hold our instant tea/coffee/chocolate/soup delivered by the vending machine. Once we've finished our drink, the cup goes into the waste bin. Imagine how many of these vending machines there must be in workplaces and leisure venues throughout the UK. Then imagine how many of those cups are thrown away in one day, one week, one month, one year.

From Ed's business you can buy a pencil. Imprinted on the side of this pencil you will find a message, which could read: 'I used to be a discarded plastic cup.' That discarded plastic cup has gone from being something nobody wanted to starting a new life as a useful product – and one with an appealing message.

Ed says he has created a business that thrills him: a business that makes a profit, provides employment for himself, provides useful employment for others and helps to preserve the world's resources. To anyone who will listen he will tell them that creating a business with social aims gives him a wonderful feeling. But there's one thing he doesn't understand. He doesn't understand why more people don't do it.

So what about you?

CHAPTER 8
THE IDEA IS IN FRONT OF YOU

Part One of this book introduces you to some process you could go through, or some technique you could apply, to come up with an idea for starting a business. But other people – and even perhaps places – can also present you with that idea you are looking for.

A DAY OUT

Fancy an interesting and enjoyable day out at low cost? One that could see you come home at the end of the day with that business idea you've been looking for.

Almost every trade and industry boasts its own periodic get-together. At these trade exhibitions and fairs you will find dozens, possibly hundreds, of trade exhibitors. In addition to the big national exhibitions you also can track down smaller regional events. At these trade shows you are likely to find importers, exporters from overseas, manufacturers, wholesalers and all kinds of suppliers of products and services ancillary to that trade. Here you might find a supplier whose products you would like to distribute, especially something you have never seen before. Very often at trade shows a manufacturer or importer will launch a new product on the market, giving you the opportunity to 'get in on the ground floor' with something different.

So, whatever trade you might be interested in entering, find out about the trade shows. One way to do this is through trade journals – which we'll be looking at later in this chapter – since often it's the journals that sponsor these events.

THE HIGH STREET

You can have an enjoyable day out doing valuable research closer to home: at the shops. You are banned from taking a shopping list with you because you won't be going as a shopper – but as an observer. Visit the stores that interest you, whose products you like, but spend time too in stores you would not normally go into. What are you looking out for? Well…almost anything.

Obviously it's useful to learn about what products are hot with a growing number of buyers in case it strikes you there's a market with room enough for one more entrant. Or some trend or some fashion might start you thinking in a certain direction. And you can learn from the techniques of successful retailers.

Rhys set up a business wholesaling pet foods. He specialised in dry complete dog feeds, supplying them in bulk to boarding kennels and dog rescue societies. He picked up an idea for promoting his product to help launch his business, from a product promotion he'd admired at Currys, the electrical retail chain. Thus he took inspiration for wholesaling a product in his own trade from what a retailer was doing in a completely different trade.

Visiting a store you wouldn't normally go into may lead you to thinking about products you wouldn't otherwise have considered.

BROWSE THE BOOK STORE

Earlier we mentioned how books and, therefore, book stores and libraries can be a valuable source of business ideas. So wander off the high street, down the side streets, to find the little independent bookshops that still exist in towns and cities. The small bookshop can be a goldmine for a prospector of business ideas.

This is because a small independent bookshop will often stock books that reflect the interests of the proprietor. The shop won't be big enough to have a stock that is representative of all types of books, so what will it concentrate on? If the owner is interested in antiques, you're likely to find a large stock of books on antiques. If their interest is food, then perhaps you'll find a huge array of books on how to cook, recipes, food manufacturing, confectionery, drinks, regional and local foods and ethnic dishes – many of which you wouldn't find even in the biggest library. And there might be a stock of second-hand books – just what you need for turning up some object from times past that you could reproduce. Such as some lost recipe you bring to light to include in your exciting new range of speciality foods.

If you like books, then you have a real advantage in your search for a business idea.

THE WORLD OF TRADE JOURNALS

Of course you don't just read books, you also read journals and newspapers. Newspapers can be a valuable source of business ideas, reporting changes in the world that can be a source of opportunities. But so, too, can journals – trade journals, that is.

Almost every trade or industry will have a publication dedicated to it. Many trades also have a journal devoted specifically to a section of that trade. For example, in the food industry you will find dozens of weekly or fortnightly or monthly journals aimed specifically at the convenience food retailer or the delicatessen or the market gardener or confectionery manufacturing.

It's here that you'll find trade news, for example about new products being launched on the market, and also trade advertising that can be of interest to you. The issue you pick up may include advertisements seeking stockists or distributors or agents for a product. If it's of interest, get in touch.

And here's a tip based on experience: don't just follow up those advertisements which are clearly of interest to you. Make the effort to get trade price lists and catalogues and visit the websites of any trade advertiser you feel might just *possibly* be of interest. Our experience is that often what you consider to be the most interesting possibility turns out to be a disappointment, while something else that you felt was probably a waste of time turns out to be worth taking further. Business – and life – is like that!

An easy way to discover what journals are out there is via one of the directories that lists them – the best-known of which is *Willings Press Guide*, available in your local library.

One monthly publication, *The Trader*, mentioned earlier, covers a range of trades. Within the pages of this interesting journal you'll find hundreds of offerings from importers, wholesalers and manufacturers of clothes, stationery, electrical goods, giftware, furniture, textiles, jewellery, watches, toys and bodycare products.

INSPIRATION FROM OTHER PEOPLE

Let's get some inspiration from what others have done – from their success.

We suggest you look at successful small business start-ups and see what you can learn from them. You could of course study any successful business, including market leaders, but the chances are that you haven't got their capital resources. Another resource that's limited is time and the most fruitful use of that limited resource for you would be to look at recent, small-scale start-ups. The capital resources involved in setting up these may be within your reach and, as recent start-ups, they may be exploiting current trends or factors that you can cash in on.

You've already started your collection of start-up successes with the case histories featured in this book. Local newspapers can also be good sources of articles about new businesses in your area, and you should get your hands on local papers from other areas. So ask Auntie Mary and Uncle Jack who live in Eastbourne to keep their copies of the *Eastbourne Gazette* for you, or check their websites. Most national and regional newspapers have business sections featuring successful businesses: cut them out to add to your collection. Most counties have their own glossy monthly journal and these can be another source of articles featuring small businesses.

As you read about what others have done there are a number of possibilities to turn over in your mind.

First, could you adopt this successful business idea? Here we have wandered into legal considerations. The basic proposition in our free enterprise society is that, if somebody has come up with an original business idea and set up a business, then you are entitled to set up in competition making use of the same idea. *Elizabeth*, a young single mum with two children, was pleased to get a write-up in her local paper about the business she had founded two years previously. This was a contract cleaning business with a difference. Her company specialised in the cleaning of newly built properties; cleaning up after the builders had moved out required special expertise. One of the newspaper's readers was *Lee*, who had previously worked in the building industry and had some industry contacts. He decided to use these contacts to start a new business – providing a specialist contract-cleaning service to builders, which involved cleaning newly built properties after the builders had moved out!

There are of course many forms of legal protection that might be relevant when you are taking inspiration from what others have done. If you have the tiniest doubt about whether your plans would tread upon somebody else's legal toes, then seek the appropriate professional advice. The most likely legal problem you could face is an allegation that you have passed off your new enterprise as being the original enterprise from which you took inspiration. The most common reason for this is confusion of name. So if you were setting up a small business retailing underwear and socks you would be advised not to call your business *Marks and Spencer*. And avoid trying to be clever: call your business Murks and Sponcer and you are still likely to receive a letter from solicitors acting for Marks and Spencer. Would a reasonable person be confused by your choice of name? If so, you might find yourself accounting to the original business for any profits you have received.

One of the authors, Barrie, holds a law degree and is a former law lecturer. His knowledge of law proved a powerful weapon when dealing with difficult customers and unreliable suppliers in his business. His view is that anybody setting up and running a business should acquire at least a fundamental knowledge of the law relating to business operations, in particular contract law and consumer law. At the very least, if you are considering taking inspiration from someone else's business idea, you should get acquainted with forms of legal protection that could be relevant, such as patents and design copyright. There are many books on the market dealing with the law relating to small businesses; we recommend you treat yourself to one.

In what other way might somebody else's business start-up success be of help to you? We suggest you look at it through a magnifying glass. Why is this business successful? Peer closely into it to identify and analyse the elements that have helped it to succeed. Can you use some of these same elements yourself?

Ask yourself: what motivates customers to buy from this business? After all, it's successful because it's got customers. Try to discover the psychological reasons why customers buy from this enterprise. If you can stand in the shoes of the customer and understand what is motivating them to hand over their money, then you could be unearthing priceless business intelligence.

Hayley was in the third year of studying art and design. She'd been very attracted to her particular course and had enrolled even though it involved her living over a hundred miles from home. Hayley had been thinking about the possibility of setting up her own business when she finished her course.

One week the free local paper in her college town carried a feature about a small business which had just celebrated its fifth birthday. Its product was reproductions of children's rocking horses from Edwardian times. Customers admired the quality of the product with its real horsehair mane and tail, leather saddle and craftsmanship. Hayley's eyebrows shot up when she read that the company had full order books for a product with an average price of £2,000.

Her grandfather had recently taken early retirement. His hobby had always been making nice objects from wood and he was now finding himself with too much time on his hands and not enough pension to pursue his hobby as he would like.

After moving back home at the end of her course Hayley joined forces with her grandfather and set up…a business making and retailing reproduction children's rocking horses.

What induces customers to pay thousands of pounds for a reproduction of a children's toy from times past? What are they really buying? Part of the attraction of this product for some buyers is that it arouses feelings of nostalgia. But probably of even greater pulling power is that it's a product that will not be thrown away.

We live in an age of mass production, which has brought great benefit to the population of developed countries, supplying us with the things we need to live our lives comfortably, at affordable prices. But mass production is inconsistent with individuality: the product is made for everybody and not just for you. So there's a huge attraction in a product made in small numbers: your neighbour may have the same car as you but it's unlikely he or she will have the same rocking horse.

And today we are constantly being encouraged to reduce, recycle and repair. Yet, as we all know from experience, many products continue to be made to have only a short lifespan. Around the home and the workplace numerous examples of throwaway products can still be found. Until recently, one of the authors was guilty of using a ballpoint pen for which no refills were available: when the ink was depleted the whole pen was consigned to the waste bin. But Hayley's rocking horse will not have a short lifespan. And it most certainly won't soon find itself in a black plastic sack. It will not be thrown away – ever. This is something that the buyer will keep and hand on to their children, who in turn will hand it on to their children. This is not just a reproduction of a children's toy; this is a family heirloom.

In our throwaway age there is something magnetically appealing about an exquisite product that will stay with you and your family and your descendants. Can you come up with an idea for a version of a product that people buy to keep? Yes you can! Get thinking!

Sometimes a business is successful and it's not all down to the proprietor's efforts. When you set up a business there will be matters affecting the business that are within your control. For example, if you open a retail outlet you can decide whether you close at 5 p.m. or 5:30 p.m. But there will be other factors that are outside your control. For example, you can't control what the government does, although what the government does can affect your business. And almost certainly, unless you are a well-known personality, you can't affect public opinion. Yet such factors, external to your business and beyond your control, could help your business to succeed.

Say you set up as a supplier of meat-free alternatives and a few weeks after your launch there was a national scare about the safety of beef – a new outbreak of mad-cow disease that sent sales of beef plummeting. Then sales of your chilled beef-style pies took off as consumers tried your alternatives. And consumers found them so tasty that, when the scare died down, a profitable percentage of those buyers stayed with your meat-free alternative.

Can you identify any external factors that might have contributed to the success of a small business? Can you come up with an idea that exploits that same external factor?

IMPROVING SERVICES

We've established that you can take inspiration from other people's success and what they have done well, but you can also take inspiration from what people don't do well.

As you use the services of other people ask yourself: 'Could I do this?' Then ask yourself: 'Could I do this better?' And think back to services you have used in the past and ask the same questions. (If you don't have all the necessary skills, could you acquire them? Or hire somebody who has them? Or take a partner?)

So many small businesses – and some not-so-small ones – have a poor public image. Consumer advice centres testify to the number of complaints directed against suppliers of everyday services. Some types of supplier are notorious: you've probably seen on TV consumer programmes horror stories about builders, garages, plumbers. Lack of public trust has resulted in a change in traditional working practices. Reports from some areas of the UK tell of women who have successfully set up in business in the building trade, formerly a male preserve. Women decorators, plumbers, electricians and carpenters are said to have been singularly successful. Many of these new businesses have quickly built a reputation for service. It seems many customers are confident that tradeswomen are less likely to tread dirt into the carpet with size 10 boots and are more likely to clear up after themselves. If you are thinking of setting up a service for which there is a need, don't necessarily be put off by the existing competition. The quality provided by many of these businesses may be so poor that you can come up with a way to improve on their service.

We've set out in Appendix 6 a list of commonplace needs met by providing a service or providing a product with a big service element. Appendix 7 sets out services that businesses frequently require. Talk to existing users of the services. Ask them: 'How could we do it better?'

People – places – events – trends – so much is out there: you could come face to face with a business idea.

CHAPTER 9
THE GRID APPROACH

Our next approach to coming up with an idea for a business is rather different in character from what we've suggested so far. Some of the ones we've already mentioned require a high dose of creativity, but the grid approach is more mechanistic.

The number of different approaches you can take is increasing and hopefully your list of possible ideas is starting to grow. Remember, the surest way to come up with a good idea is to have loads of ideas. And if you're feeling weary with all the effort you've put in, it's a good time to remind you of the number one characteristic of positive entrepreneurs from our old friend Percy Verance: keep at it.

The grid approach is a simple technique for you to use and it involves the use of two lists. The first is a list of the ways in which a business can meet customers. Very often, when we ask a budding entrepreneur who's come up with a product they want to retail how they will meet customers, we get a standard reply. 'I'll have to get shop premises' is the answer we get from the minority who are lucky enough to have sufficient funds to rent premises. 'I'll take a stall on the Saturday market' is the reply from many others. These are the most obvious channels if you are selling to the general public, but there are many other possibilities for reaching customers and some of these involve very small start-up costs and low ongoing overheads.

We also want to remind you here about one of your answers in the *Who am I?* questionnaire. We asked you what sort of business you would like to run, whether you'd prefer to deal with people face to face or via the computer and whether you'd like to be out and about or are happy to spend your days in an office from nine until five. These matters should be borne in mind as we go through our list of possible channels to customers. So keep asking yourself: would this method of meeting customers suit me?

1. At home

Some products and services have to be sold direct to the customer in the home because it is necessary for the supplier to see the premises. An obvious example is the interior decorator who needs to visit the premises to work out the time and the materials that will be involved.

Barrie's business supplying suite covers, set up after he was made redundant, is another example. Some furniture is not suitable for covers, and in all potential sales Barrie would need to see the suite to work out how much fabric was involved and how complex it would be to produce covers tailor-made for the suite.

We recently compiled a list of some 40 products and services that are sold to the customer in the home. These range from the most obvious and common examples such as home improvements, including conservatories, replacement windows, fitted kitchens and bathrooms, through to distance-learning courses. The latter is an example of a service where it is not essential to visit the customer at home, but doing so may offer a better service; in this instance it offers prospective students the chance to have one-to-one counselling in the privacy of their own home.

Can you come up with a product or service where it is not essential to visit the customer in their home but, by doing so, you'd be offering a benefit the competition does not?

2. Through the post

Despite the rise in Internet shopping there are still plenty of mail-order businesses operating in the traditional manner via catalogues, mailshots and newspaper/magazine advertisements, although many of these businesses now augment their sales with a web presence.

Two particular types of market lend themselves well to a mail-order operation. A scattered market is one where, although there are buyers for a product in any given area, these are unlikely to be enough for a supplier to justify having a physical presence in the form of high-street premises. A collectors' market is one example: there might not be enough collectors of, say, US stamps to warrant your having retail premises, but if you could reach every collector of US stamps in the UK you might have enough customers for a small business. Remember, a small business can live off a small market.

Another example of a small market that could be served by a mail-order business is one with customers who only make infrequent purchases. An example is a manufacturer of cups, shields and other awards that are given out by schools, sports clubs and other societies, probably only once a year. In a small town this probably wouldn't amount to sufficient business to justify the overheads of retail premises, but if you put all those infrequent purchasers throughout the UK together, you'd have a sizeable market.

Of course, both scattered buyers and infrequent buyers can be reached today via the Internet.

3. www.mybusiness

Up to now we've deliberately not given a great deal of prominence to the possibility that your business could be an e-business because, in our experience, too many young people rely on the Internet, either exclusively or at least too much, to provide their business idea. Yes, the volume of goods and services sold this way has grown explosively over the last decade, but the following considerations should be borne in mind.

According to the latest figures, over 90 per cent of goods and services are not purchased on the Internet; they are sold through the other channels we're looking at in this chapter. Now, we're not trying to deter you from setting up an e-business. It could be that your skills and interests point you in the direction of an Internet-based operation. Or perhaps you're considering setting up a business that reaches customers through a more traditional route but which augments its sales by having a web presence too. A note of caution, though: many of the most successful sites are operated by household name suppliers who also have a high-street presence. Names such as Argos, Tesco and Comet spring to mind: a good proportion of Internet sales is generated by these traditional bricks and mortar retailers.

It might be that you come up with an idea for an Internet business that takes the world by storm, such as eBay or Facebook, one which exploits the capabilities of the Web – and turns you in to a multimillionaire. There are also certain types of product that lend themselves particularly well to having an Internet presence. Certainly, the more unusual or esoteric the product, the more you should consider reaching out across the globe through your own website.

Let's suppose you had an interest in history and your idea was to manufacture reproductions of weapons from times past. We'd presume the market was tiny, but that there was nevertheless a market. Buyers might include members of those associations that re-enact historical battles, such as (in the UK) the Sealed Knot. So if you are planning to set up manufacturing reproductions of, say, 12th-century spears, you should engage the services of a web designer as soon as possible.

As mentioned earlier, if you come up with a product that really is different from anything that's gone before, it can take the market some time to adjust and to understand the benefits of this product. Buyers can be slow to adapt and to give up buying what they are accustomed to. However, there are buyers with a certain type of personality who are more willing to try something new on the market – many of these are younger buyers – and research suggests that such buyers are heavier-than-average users of the Internet. So if you do come up with a product that is a radical departure from what has gone before, your first priority should be to build a website.

Then there's eBay, of course. We cautioned you earlier about having a narrow vision and concentrating exclusively on the Internet as your route to business, but we must confess we've been impressed by the number of entrepreneurs – many of them young people – who have used eBay to build from scratch businesses which now have a considerable turnover. With eBay, there are so many possibilities and it's such a phenomenon that it deserves a book to itself. There are a number of titles that deal exclusively with doing business on eBay and we've included a couple of these in our further reading list in Appendix 3.

The feedback system on eBay enables you to gauge the volume of business a particular seller is enjoying; some of these are businesses with enviable turnovers. With no costly overheads for high-street premises, and access to buyers throughout the UK and overseas, you can be up and running within days. However, there are some 'buts'. Firstly, eBay can be very price competitive: it's a simple matter for the buyer of a standard product to compare prices from competing suppliers. Against that, it may be possible to work on higher margins with products that aren't so easy to compare, such as jewellery. Also, with some items there is an element of competition between buyers: this might be true of, say, a collectors' market. And in a collectors' market you might have an object with comparative rarity value, which will help push up your price: by offering it through eBay you will be getting exposure to thousands of potential buyers for your picture postcard or 18th-century coin or ornamental frog.

As a sixth-form student, Cherrelle found that the income from her part-time job wasn't going to be enough to pay for the two-week holiday in the Caribbean she wanted to book. To help with her holiday savings she decided to put some of her stuff on eBay.

After she'd cleared out the items she no longer wanted, her takings from these encouraged her to risk a little of the money she'd brought in. She would pick up items at car-boot fairs that she felt might fetch a higher price on eBay. Her first offering as a trader was a second-hand Tri-ang railway set purchased from a car-boot seller who was clearing out his deceased aunt's house. Cherrelle was surprised by the number of bids from buyers in the last minute of the auction.

Her interest in sport and fitness led her to purchasing from a supplier – found in The Trader – customer returns of fitness equipment. Some of this needed repacking and occasionally some dismantling but, at an average purchase price of 10 per cent of retail price, there was plenty of margin left to cover the costs of selling on eBay. The continuing public interest in fitness and reducing obesity – coupled with a desire for a bargain – saw Cherrelle with a business which, in 12 months, had grown to sales of over 100 items per week. Such was the volume of business that she decided to take a gap year between sixth-form college and university to see just how far her business could grow...

4. Party plan

Selling products by hosting a party or social event is a very low-cost way into business, although it's true to say that many party plan operations are part-time businesses. It's another way of avoiding costly overheads for high-street premises and an example of going out to where people are. There are of course some big-name operators in party plan, including Virgin and The Body Shop, both offering the types of products that can work well with a party plan operation, i.e. something to demonstrate and something to try on. Party plan is a much bigger business in the US than in the UK and that may be something to do with the culture. But if you're interested in this as a way of getting business, again there are books devoted solely to this type of operation and you'll find a couple of these titles in Appendix 3.

THE CUSTOMER'S WORKPLACE

If a business has retail premises, it is likely to have passing trade – people going by the door who may be attracted into the store. As we've seen, party plan is an example of going to where people are rather than waiting for them to come to you; and so is our next suggestion. What about taking your product to potential customers at their place of work? It's done already with books, toys, novelties, greetings cards and stationery, all of which are products that lend themselves to browsing: something for employees to do in their lunch break or coffee break. Often the goods, displayed in the firm's foyer or staffroom, are offered at a discount but this method of getting your products to potential customers can also work well with lines employees are not likely to see in the supermarket, such as novelties. How many of the employees who will see your attractive display have friends and relatives with birthdays or anniversaries coming up for whom they'll want to buy a present? Your alligator stapler could be just what they are looking for!

YOUR AGENTS

Today, more and more people need additional sources of income. This includes students, whose numbers have grown hugely in recent years, and people pushed into early retirement who have found that their scaled-down pension does not give them the lifestyle they had planned for. Yet most part-time jobs are not the route to riches: waiting on tables or working behind the bar is likely to be rewarded with the minimum wage. Perhaps these part-time workers could earn more not as employees but as sales agents. A sales agent is someone who represents a business and makes sales on its behalf.

CASE STUDY

Since leaving school three years ago Dan had worked for a company who manufactured wood products for the garden, including sheds and summerhouses. Although he didn't undergo an apprenticeship, during his time with the business he learnt enough to feel confident that he could make similar products in partnership with a mate who was also fed up with his job and interested in starting a business.

Dan had the skills to make the product – but how to get sales? Approaches to garden centres locally were unsuccessful because they were content with their existing suppliers. National chains of DIY outlets would need supplies in bigger quantities than Dan could cope with.

Dan's eventual route to customers was through a network of agents. The earnings for each agent were likely to be modest and would therefore only suit people looking for a part-time activity to supplement their existing income. The classified advertisement in the agent's local paper included the agent's telephone number. Interested customers could see sample products displayed in the agent's garden and take away a catalogue, produced on an ink-jet printer, showing the full range of products. Since each agent had no overheads to meet, the commission paid to them on each sale was far lower than the profit a garden centre would expect. This enabled Dan to offer his products at prices that undercut the garden centres and so were attractive to potential buyers seeking a discounted product.

There would be outlay for the samples and sales literature your agents required, but some of these costs might be offset by asking agents to provide a refundable deposit.

So what could you supply to customers through your team of agents?

MORE CHANNELS...

Some routes to customers may not in themselves provide enough customers for a full-time business, so perhaps you could combine two of the remaining possibilities.

One possibility – and yet another example of going out to the customer – is to take your product to the retirement market. Here's a group of potential customers, possibly scores of them in one place, who might be pleased to see your display of goods at their sheltered housing complex or residential home or day centre. If, as a young person, the grey market does not appeal to you, perhaps we can make it more appealing by pointing out that many retired people currently enjoy final-salary pensions, which gives them a greater income than that of young people in full-time employment. Bear in mind, too, that nearly all of these potential customers don't have mortgages to pay or kids to support. With more and more of us living longer, it's a growing market. If your initial reaction was that the retirement market is not one for you, then we'd advise you to think again!

Could you go out to schools and hospitals and other providers of public services to meet customers? We know of a major hospital which has 5,000 staff and 50,000 patients a year. Its concourse boasts a number of shops, including high-street names, but also a number of kiosks and stalls rented out to small businesses. It's another example of what could be a potentially profitable outlet for the small business in the gift trade. On a recent visit to this hospital one of the authors was struck by the number of visitors crowding round a stall retailing a range of watches all at one price: £5. He counted 12 potential customers browsing, one customer paying for their purchase and a further customer waiting to be served. A business in a hospital! But then many providers of public services need to boost their income, and allowing traders on to their premises is a way of doing this. We also know of a small business that makes regular visits to the staff at a police headquarters. So where could you take your product?

The gift trade also provided us recently with an interesting example of a wholesale business. This enterprise, set up two years ago, has a mobile showroom that visits gift shops and other retail outlets with gift lines, such as card shops. Since the overwhelming majority of gift shops are small independent businesses, the proprietor is likely to be working at the business and therefore available to see the sales representative and view the products in the mobile showroom. Compare that with trying to get to see the buyer at a household name high-street retailer!

Or could you use wheels to provide a delivery service direct to customers in the home? Older people may find the time comes when it's not easy for them to get out and about but not all their needs can be met by the supermarket's home delivery service. One successful business, which started some three years ago, delivers pet foods of all kinds to householders. Many dog and cat foods today take the form of dry feedstuffs sold in bulk. This can represent a saving on the price of tinned pet foods but there's the disadvantage of weight: lugging money-saving, 15-kilo sacks of dog food is not something you look forward to when you are 80 years old. But you might look forward to the regular monthly call from your friendly pet-food delivery person – who, if you live alone, might be the only person you talk to that day. A growing need and a growing market.

Vicky, whose jewellery and hair accessories business we looked at earlier, found a new outlet in her second year of trading: she contacts clubs, societies and other social groups asking if she can attend their meetings with an attractive display of her range. She finds this works particularly well from September onwards when the 40 or 50 or 60 members of the Ladies Circle are thinking about Christmas presents…

CONSTRUCTING YOUR GRID

Hopefully, at least one of these various routes to the customer will have appealed to you. An outgoing personality like you might, for instance, enjoy demonstrating your product at sales parties. Or perhaps the thought of the quick start that an eBay business could give you is luring you towards your computer. Or maybe it would suit you to get out and about, calling into offices and other workplaces. What is your product line to be?

Look again at your answers to the question in your *Who am I?* questionnaire that asked you to list the products you are interested in. Possibly you overlooked something, so as a memory jogger here's a list of some popular product lines:

- accessories, e.g. sunglasses
- bicycles
- CDs
- clothing
- computers and accessories
- cosmetics and bodycare products
- DVDs
- electrical goods
- fitness equipment
- food
- furniture
- garden products
- gift lines
- hair accessories
- hardware
- household textiles
- jewellery
- leather goods
- luggage
- novelty lines
- shoes

- sports equipment
- sportswear
- tools
- toys
- watches

Take a sheet of paper and list down the left-hand side the product ranges that interest you. Hopefully, there are at least a few of these. Then at the top of the sheet, across the page, write the 'channels to customers' that appeal to you.

Your sheet may look something like the following:

	Party plan	Agents	Delivery service
Sportswear	───────────────────────────────		
Cosmetics	───────────────────────────────		
Bodycare	───────────────────────────────		
Tools	───────────────────────────────		
Jewellery	───────────────────────────────		

Working your way down the list of product ranges that appeal to you, take each one in turn and ask whether it lends itself to any of the channels to customers you've listed at the top of the sheet. If so, on the line for that product range place a ✓ in the appropriate column. Once you have worked your way down the list it may look like the following.

	Party plan	Agents	Delivery service
Sportswear	✗	✓	✗
Cosmetics	✓	✗	✓
Bodycare	✓	✓	✗
Tools	✗	✓	✓
Jewellery	✓	✓	✗

What this process should reveal is a product that you like and/or are interested in and a way of meeting customers that appeals to you. So if the plan you drew up corresponded with the example above, it would reveal that you might consider setting up a business retailing jewellery via party plan. Of course, you would then have to decide what type of jewellery this should be. But the process will have given you a product range and a route to customers for you to consider.

So fetch that pen and paper!

CHAPTER 10
A BUSINESS IN A BOX

Let's be frank: the overwhelming majority of people reading this book will of course have some doubts about whether they should start their own business. Some of these doubts will be down to a lack of support from family and friends. And, some of these doubts may also be asserting themselves because you weren't a shining star at school or college – you didn't get five As at A level. If this is you, remind yourself that some of the most successful entrepreneurs in the world can't spell.

But other doubts may spring from lack of experience – you haven't set up your own business before. It's always daunting to do something for the first time. Yes, you'll have much to learn. But you've got this book to help you and there's lots of other help and support available to you.

That said, this will almost certainly be the first business you set up, so you might feel more relaxed about it if, instead of starting up from scratch, you took up what we call a business in a box. We use this term to cover a number of possibilities, but what these businesses have in common is that you will be following a path that's been trail-blazed by somebody else, doing what they're doing, and with their help in some form or other.

You can find out about these business opportunity packages from a number of sources. The business sections of national, regional and local newspapers often carry advertisements for business opportunities, as do a number of general publications, such as *Exchange & Mart*. We suggested earlier that you find out about trade journals. If you look through these you will see they often carry advertisements for business opportunities. And today the Internet has countless websites offering alluring opportunities – quite possibly, you have already at some time or other received spam e-mail inviting you to visit one of these money-making websites. You'll find that if you respond to some business opportunities announcement, whether it's on the Web or elsewhere, you'll soon be receiving communications by e-mail and post from other promoters of business opportunities. Your name and address will soon go on a mailing list which is sold on to promoters of money-making schemes.

Much of what you see and read, whether it's on a website or in a glossy brochure you've been sent, will strike you as over the top. We never cease to be amazed by the claims and style of some of the material. Letters, brochures, web pages proclaiming a MASSIVE money-making opportunity in an EXPLOSIVE market. And so often you're told that you will miss out unless you respond immediately: you must take URGENT action. The offer is TIME-SENSITIVE.

After contacting an advertiser in a Sunday newspaper, one of the authors received an offer promising '£2,000-plus every week for no more than five hours' work'. In case he had doubts about setting up a business which would immediately return him £400 an hour, the brochure went on to reassure him that earnings of £400 an hour were not fictional. The advertiser guaranteed it. And he was told 'the business is so simple a child could operate it'.

A website offering a business opportunity – from America – tells us that there is no catch in it. An amazing new discovery will earn us '£4,000 per month for a total of 40 minutes' work'. And that £4,000 will be tax free. That works out at £100 a minute. Who could pass that up? Of course, these opportunities will require an 'investment' on our part.

You must be wondering: does anybody take offers couched in such terms seriously? We're afraid the answer is 'yes'. Selling business opportunities is big business – especially when unemployment is high.

But you're much too mature and intelligent to get taken in by something that's too good to be true.

When you reply to advertisements for business opportunities, what you are offered will take a number of forms, as outlined below.

AGENCIES AND DISTRIBUTORSHIPS

In Chapter 9 we looked at the possibility of your new business reaching its customers via a network of agents. We saw that an agent is a person who acts on behalf of another and a common type of agent is the sales agent. Now we will consider the possibility that it is you who will act as the agent – for another business. Many trades use sales agents, and trade journals often carry advertisements seeking agents. From the point of view of a manufacturer or importer of goods, the use of agents can have advantages over having a team of sales representatives who are full-time employees. Chief amongst these is the possibility of lower costs, since agents are paid on a commission basis: no sale, no commission to pay. Contrast that with the need to provide an employee with a monthly salary credit, no matter that sales are poor.

Some advertisers seek 'distributors' for their goods. In practice, the terms 'agent' and 'distributor' are sometimes used loosely by business people to mean the same thing. A distributor is likely to hold stock of the supplier's line and sell the product direct to their own customers. By contrast, if you are a genuine agent – and haven't been misnamed – then the sale that you bring about will be between the customer and the supplier you are representing (termed in law the 'principal'). Here the contract (of sale) is between the supplier and the customer; the agent is merely an intermediary. This means that the legal responsibilities under the contract of sale and under consumer law lie primarily with the supplier and not the agent.

BUSINESS FORMULAE

When you respond to advertisements for business opportunities, you'll often find that the supplier is offering to sell you information. In return for your credit card details they will let you in on a secret idea for a business for you to set up, together with information on how to operate the business. The advertiser will tempt you by setting out the benefits this secret idea will bring you. It's common for these benefits to include no requirement for skills, no need for previous experience, you can start it for the price of a few pints of beer and customers will be banging on your door, etc. There is of course an element of gambling in taking up one of these offers: even if the extravagant claims were true, the business might turn out to be a type that didn't appeal to you. One gentlemen of our acquaintance paid £40 for a business manual that divulged an idea promising the benefits listed above. He decided not to pursue the business when page three of the manual revealed the idea was the making of pornographic videos.

Likely to be of greater use are offers to supply information about how to run a business, the idea itself being revealed before you commit to purchase the know-how.

CASE STUDY

Abebi purchased a manual on how to set up and run a business in the pet-food trade; the advertisement making it clear that a pet-food home delivery service was the business idea. The author of the 40-page manual, which cost £30, had himself set up and operated such a business successfully for some years. The manual revealed both the benefits and the pitfalls of running such a business, including tried and tested techniques for promoting it, insider information about how to boost profit margins, plus trade secrets revealing the most profitable sources of supply.

Abebi, who bought the manual after responding to an advertisement in *Exchange & Mart*, was so impressed by the quality of the information provided she decided this would be the business she set up.

Be forewarned that many of these publications come from the US. A business idea which has taken off in one culture may not necessarily take root in another. You may also find that the material provided, whether produced in the UK or abroad, has been padded out with general information on setting up a business. Much of this will not be of the slightest relevance to you if the information was written for the US market. To read page after page about the legal regulations for setting up in Oklahoma will be of no help if you are setting up in Cleethorpes.

MULTI-LEVEL MARKETING

This is a somewhat controversial form of business. Also known as network marketing, it is often confused with 'pyramid schemes'. Some years ago, many people looking for a business opportunity got their fingers burnt with these pyramid schemes. Entrants to the scheme would buy a stock of a product that they were then to resell, and their profit on the stock would be greater the more they purchased. Having been lured into buying more stock than they could sell, thousands of people ended up with garages full of unsold items.

Multi-level marketing activities (MLM for short) are subject to legal regulation about the maximum investment that can be made, among other matters. Many business opportunity ads turn out to be from MLM distributors seeking to recruit others to join their network. Profits come from two sources. Firstly, as a distributor you make profit on the sales of the product to friends, relatives, neighbours and other acquaintances. Secondly, you can earn by recruiting others to make sales too. You will of course receive a payment from the company for the sales made by the people in your 'downline'.

There are numerous reputable companies who reach their customers through a network marketing scheme. Many of these established companies have turnovers running into tens of millions of pounds. In particular, MLM suits consumable products – i.e. those which get used up regularly – thus providing distributors with repeat orders. Bodycare products and health supplements are prime examples.

Many people become MLM distributors thanks to dreams of great wealth generated by enormous earnings. It is undoubtedly true that some established companies have numerous longstanding distributors with six-figure annual earnings. But as one such distributor told us: 'This wasn't get-rich-quick. This was get rich slowly, because of the hours and effort I've had to put in. I've worked 12 hours a day, six days a week to build up and train my downline.' But then many of the people in his downline will be happy to run a tiny operation, content with selling modest quantities of their product to friends and relatives, not wishing to have the responsibility of managing, motivating and training others.

Reputable MLM companies are members of the professional body, the Direct Selling Association (DSA). The DSA website (**www.dsa.org.uk**) includes a list of member companies and contact details.

FRANCHISES

If you're feeling *very* nervous about starting your own business and are particularly lacking in self-confidence, then taking up a franchise might appeal to you. This can be a very safe route into business. You purchase the right to do what somebody else is already doing: to use their established name and copy their successful way of doing business. Many household name companies run franchise operations, especially in the food industry. The professional body for franchise companies is the British Franchise Association (**www.thebfa.org**); join a BFA company as a franchisee and you probably have a 90 per cent chance of it succeeding. So why isn't everybody who wants their own business taking on a franchise?

With the best-known franchise operations, the costs may cause you to forget any thoughts of becoming a franchisee. A fast-food outlet in the high-street could set you back six figures-plus. Many providers of services to households are franchise operations, but even here, with no costly premises involved, you could be looking at a fee of £20,000 or more to become a franchisee.

It is possible, though, that you might be offered a franchise where entry costs are more modest, perhaps a couple of thousand pounds. But you have to ask yourself what you are getting for this. With an established franchise operation from a major franchisor you will have the benefit of trading under an established brand name. Set up a Kentucky Fried Chicken (KFC) outlet and your potential customers will know exactly what they'll be getting. And you will be getting support from a company with an established track record in its field. But not all franchise operations are equal.

CASE STUDY

Mark's first attempt at being his own boss hadn't worked out. At the age of 20, together with a mate, he had opened a mobile phone store in the small market town where he lived. Price competition from Internet sellers and supermarkets, combined with the rent and other overheads for his high-street premises, saw the business struggle for two years before Mark and his partner decided to call it a day.

This lack of success at his first attempt at business severely dented Mark's confidence. But he had in many ways enjoyed being his own boss and was reluctant to return to a nine-to-five routine and being told what to do by others. Maybe a franchise would give him a greater chance of business success.

A franchise opportunity costing only £3,000 seemed tempting. The fee, according to the franchisor's brochure, was 'covered by stock'. He would receive £3,000-worth of stock, at trade price, which he would then sell on to customers. Mark was about to sign up but decided to give the matter a little more thought. And the more he thought about it the more he could see the benefit…for the franchise company. Over the next few weeks he received several phone calls from the company's sales director but he couldn't persuade Mark to sign on the dotted line.

When deciding whether or not to take up the franchise Mark put himself in the shoes of the company, the franchisor, and looked at it from their point of view. Doing this convinced him that the company, which wasn't a member of the BFA, got more benefit from the deal than did the franchisee. In effect, he'd be buying £3,000-worth of stock from the company, which he would then have to sell on. Buying all this stock, of course, would give him a great incentive to get out on the road and shift it, thus making sales for the company. And if he had signed the franchise agreement, Mark would not be able to offer a competing product to his customers. So he'd have been tied down to purchasing the product he sold only from the franchise company. Again, a good deal for the company.

If you set up a successful business from scratch, perhaps as a way of expanding it you could consider offering it to others as a franchise opportunity.

And that suggestion leads us to Part Two of the book.

PART TWO:
HOW TO
MAKE IT A
SUCCESS

CHAPTER 11
YOU WANT TO DO *WHAT*?

If you've got this far in the book, then hopefully you have at least a list of *possible* ideas. Maybe you've even made the big decision and know what you are going to do. Either way, you will be setting up a business, so there is quite a lot you need to know.

Before you launch into your challenging task, we feel this is a good point to make sure you've got plenty of energy and determination. Inspirational and motivational as we want this book to be, we're not going to pretend there won't be times when you might wish you'd done something easier. Setting up and running your own business involves rather more than a job stacking shelves at the local supermarket. Whether you've got one GCSE at Grade E or a Master's degree in business, there's plenty you'll need to learn about setting up and running a business. The big difference is that if you're the one with the Master's degree it will probably come as a shock how much you still need to find out.

So let's recharge your motivation by reminding you of some of the benefits you could get from taking a path that most other people in your age group don't go down. Through the words of others who have trodden this path, let's recap what you might be seeking.

Phoebe, who set up a small cake-making business using recipes found in old recipe books, told us:

> *You're the boss. You have control. You have control over things like when you take your holidays. And with my business I've got some flexibility over my work hours.*

If you set up in business and underestimate the constraints and the difficulties, then you won't be prepared for them. But if we give you a realistic picture of what's involved, so you know what you're taking on, you'll be more likely to stick with it.

Phoebe continued:

> *Nevertheless if you're going to set up in business, you've got to realise that there are limits to how much control you have over things such as your working hours. You have to show you've got some self-discipline. In my business, I often have to work in the evening to meet orders, which means I might not be able to go out that night with my mates. I find it especially*

hard if I have to work on Friday nights getting orders ready because that was always my big night out.

So, would you give up your Friday night out? In *your* business you might not have to. Or you might be happy to do so if there were other compensations. Such as money. Here's *Nick*, who at the age of 24 set up a sales training business.

Being the boss, you ultimately have control over what you and your business can earn. When I set up my business I took it seriously. I've worked hard, putting in the hours, because by doing so I could earn good money. On the other hand if I don't put in a lot of effort I don't earn much. Some of the companies I do training for are a long way from where I live, which means those days I don't get home until late in the evenings. I could choose not to take on those clients and then I'd be home in time to go out Thursday and Friday nights – but I wouldn't be earning so much.

Once the business was off the ground, I chose to compromise. Some weeks I do the long-distance clients and other weeks I don't, which means that some weeks I can have my Thursday and Friday nights out. To me, this is what is meant by flexibility. My first job as a sales assistant was with a store with long opening hours and we used to work on a rota, so sometimes I'd have a late finish. But I was told when that would be; it wasn't for me to choose.

Being the boss, you can to some extent at least – depending on the type of business – organise your working days. Not all my days are spent with clients, I have some office days. Those days I might not decide until I start work what it is I'll do. If I'm in the mood, say, for doing some telephone marketing, then the chances are I will do it better. So that's what I'll do that day.

I haven't got somebody telling me what to do!

Nick reminds us there's a choice you might have to make – between time spent on your social life and time spent on your business. The less time spent on your business, the less money you are likely to earn. But there can also be another social life versus money dilemma.

Back to Phoebe:

Whatever your age, you have to realise that there will be things you need for your business.

One weekend, my mates were going away to celebrate a birthday and I worked out it would cost probably £200 with the hotel and travelling and spending money. But I needed a photocopier for my business and that meant a £250 deposit. As I'd only just started up, I hadn't made provision for that and so it came down to a choice between weekend away or photocopier. I like my business, so the photocopier won.

Nick also faced choices about money and one he had to make in the early days was particularly important:

I don't know if it's the same when you're older but certainly for me, at my time of life, my image was important. I think it is for most young people.

I like designer clothes. To be honest, again like most people in my age group, I like to impress my mates. When I had a job

*I spent most of my money – and I was earning good money –
on clothes. But when I set up my own business it was important
for me to get the business off the ground and working. I needed
money for that. So I spent quite a bit of money on a really nice
brochure instead of buying something new and amazing for
when I went out with my mates. I don't know whether my
mates noticed, but I did, and so my self-image took a bit of a
dent. But then once the business was off the ground, my self-
image got a real boost. And after a while I could afford the
£600 suit anyway. But the early days can bring uncomfortable
choices.*

When it comes to setting up a business, money will have a big
influence on everything, including, of course, the choice of
business. Later in the book, we'll be devoting a whole chapter to
money: we'll look at such matters as how much you'll need to set
up, how you could raise it and how much you'll need to keep
going. As we've seen, in the early days of his business Nick had
concerns about damage to the image he had so carefully built up:
the image of the guy who could always afford the best designer
clothes and stuff to go with them. Adam, who set up an American-
style ice-cream parlour, also had concerns about damage to his
image. Whatever your age, in our society the car you drive says
something about you. And for a lot of young people the car they
drive says a huge lot about them to the rest of the world.

If you've got a car your mates would like to have, how would
you feel if your earnings from your business in the early days
weren't enough for you to be able to make the payments and/or
run it? Of course, it may be that later the financial rewards your

business brings you are such that you'll be able to afford the sort of car you never thought you could. But in the meantime, Adam had this to say about the car dilemma:

> *For many young people, the car they own is a big part of their image. But setting up your own business may mean waving goodbye to your car. My business needed a lot of start-up capital to fit the premises out. Although I was lucky because my dad was a builder and could do a lot of it, money was still very, very tight. I'd only recently bought an Audi, which was the love of my life, but I needed a van for the business and no way was I going to be able to afford to run two motors, especially with the insurance. So I became the proud owner of a Transit van.*
>
> *I broke up with my girlfriend soon after. You might think I'm joking but I think that was one of the causes. When we went out somewhere, she liked to go out in a nice car, not a Transit van.*

Had it ever occurred to you before reading this book that if you set up a business you might lose your girlfriend/boyfriend because they had to ride around in a van instead of a nice car that all their mates could admire?

And since this is a handbook especially for your age group, we need to bear in mind that this is probably the time of your life when you will be at your busiest searching out a partner – and we're not talking about a business partner. When selecting your business idea, shouldn't you consider the impact it might have on your love life? You won't have the chance to meet so many young ladies or gentlemen if your business is one where you have to work evenings and/or weekends. But perhaps you're already in a steady relationship and can work evenings because you no longer go to nightclubs to collect mobile phone numbers?

But then if you *are* in a relationship, how will your other half feel about spending time on their own? And are you going out with a student whose course at uni only involves attending eight hours a week and who gets loads of free time during the day? If *you* take time off from your business during the day, you won't be earning. Then again, maybe you have chosen a business that gives you flexibility and you can work while he/she is in the lecture theatre.

Remember, you need to choose a business that suits you so you persevere with it – but it might also need to be one that suits somebody else in your life as well.

And what about your family? If you're aged 40, it's unlikely your parents will have a great deal of influence over whether you start a business or over what business you actually start and if you're 50, there's even less chance. Although, whatever your age, your parents might be a source of financial help if you can get them to lend you a few quid.

If you're 20 and starting a business, your parents are likely to have something to say about it. And if you're 17 and thinking of starting a business you're probably going to have to listen.

We've got to be blunt at this point and tell you that for some young people setting up a business, the biggest obstacle they have to overcome is the input of their parents. Even if your parents are supportive and think your setting up in business is a great idea, bear in mind that they might not be right about everything. There might even be factors influencing them that they're not aware of.

A big difference between starting a business when you're young and starting it later in life is that the younger you are, the more likely it is you'll still be living at home with your parents. This will obviously affect the degree of influence they have over you, but it can also restrict the options open to you. Let's hear what some of your predecessors had to say about this.

Gemma, who started a business as a wholesale distributor of American chocolates and other 'candy', says:

> *Like most people my age I was still living at home with my family when I decided I'd like to set up my own business.*
>
> *I realised that, as a youngster, setting up and working on my own might not be the easiest option. But I took the view that the possible benefits and end results would outweigh the effort involved in getting round any obstacles. My parents, like many other parents I guess, definitely thought that, because of my age, starting up a business would be risky.*
>
> *My dad especially was very much against it. Mum was more willing to listen and to give her support. But with my dad, it got to the stage where it was better to say as little as possible about my plans and what I was going to do, as his negative comments were starting to drain me. But, because I was living at home, it was difficult to avoid my dad's input. He knew what was going on. He knew I was going off to meetings with a business adviser from the local enterprise agency and that I was spending a lot of time writing my business plan. All the things that you do when you're trying to come up with a business idea, and then actually setting up the business, were being done from home. Under my dad's nose.*

He meant well and I didn't just dismiss his advice without thinking about it. Your parents have more experience of life than you have. And it's especially worth thinking about what they have to say when it involves people. My mum is good at weighing up other people and at one stage when I was thinking of going into partnership with a mate, I really listened to what my mum said about her.

But I'd say to anyone in my age group who was setting up in business that the older people in your life may have a more limited world experience; it's possible you know more about some things than your dad or your mum or your aunt or your uncle. My dad has lived in the same small town all his life; he's worked in the same type of job and he got married and settled down when he was young. I lived in London for a while and I went away to uni. So don't let your parents' limited experiences hold you back by persuading you to do the same as they did.

After a holiday abroad, *Kelly* had set up a business supplying a range of children's wooden toys made from sustainable sources, taking inspiration from what she'd seen in Scandinavia. When she announced she was setting up in business, her family's reaction led her to have strong views about the input of parents.

My dad's reaction was: you're going to do WHAT? Both he and my mum had always wanted me to take up a profession, be a lawyer or an accountant or something like that. But that just isn't me! You've got to realise that your personality may be completely different from your parents, and your outlook and what you want from life could also be completely different.

Your parents may not be creative like you. Or they may be conformists and worry a lot about what the neighbours will think. Their attitude towards risk could be completely different. And of course – and I hope my parents never see this because I'm not necessarily talking about them – you might be more intelligent than them.

I was 18 when I set up my business and was still living at home. Later on, when my dad accepted that this was what I was going to do, he did make some good points, ones that I listened to. He'd worked in insurance all his life and he told me about some useful things and highlighted some pitfalls to look out for and, in those instances, he knew what he was talking about. But, otherwise, what he and my mum said usually contradicted what I was told by the trainers on a business start-up course I took and also by the business counsellors I saw afterwards.

I came to realise – and I really think anyone in my age group setting up a business should take this on board – that your parents simply don't see you how the rest of the world sees you. They have a completely different view of you from that of people you meet in business. They didn't see me as I am now, as an 18-year-old with enough sense to set up her own business. They still saw me as their little girl, who not long ago was still at school.

And because, like my mum and dad, many parents will have plans and ambitions for their children, if you want to go off and do something else, then that can really cause friction. When you are growing up your parents have so much power and control over you. When you're little they can tell you what time to go to bed, what you'll have for your dinner and what time you can stay out till. As you grow up and become your own person, they start to lose control over you, even if you're still living under their roof. And, since most young people take the route of A levels or uni or an apprenticeship and don't start their own business, your parents may see the latter almost as an act of revolt or rebellion. That was certainly the case with my parents.

However, I must also add something my grandparents told me. Even if your parents are broadly in favour of the idea of you striking up on your own, the reason for an apparent lack of support or interest may be because they think that, with a lack of business experience and limited life experience, the financial risks of your setting up at your age would be too great. And that if things go wrong they'll be expected to act as a safety net and bail you out financially. So, if your parents are not as supportive as you might have expected, it could be that is what's on their mind, even if they don't say it. They might be worried that there will be money implications for them. After all, if you want to be your own boss, why should they worry about whether they might be expected to bail you out if things don't work out? So, try to put them at ease: for example, show them the figures – they may be overestimating the start-up costs involved.

One thing that really surprised me after I set up my business and it got off the ground and was doing well, was that nothing changed with my parents. At first this puzzled me, but later I realised what was happening. My business was successful and I was now proving my parents wrong. And it wasn't easy for them to admit this. So, if you have a lack of support from the family, don't expect it to change later.

If your family don't support you, or are even actively against the idea, I'd say this. We all have to be ready to be on our own at some time. Your parents won't be there for ever so there must come a point in your life where you've got to make the decisions. Think about what you want to achieve and realise you may have reached the point in life when you have to be your own person and make the decision yourself. If it's what you want to do, even if you have to do it by yourself, go for it!

Of course, your family's attitude to your announcement that you want to set up your own business will be very much affected by *your* attitude. If you make it clear from the outset that you're not going to listen to what they have to say, then you could be throwing away a possible valuable source of help. Better to have a positive attitude. And rather than announcing that you've already decided you're going to set up your own business, perhaps you should tell them that this is what you are *thinking* of doing. If you approach others – who could be a source of help – on the basis that you are seeking their advice and their input, they are likely to feel flattered and better disposed towards helping you.

This softly-softly approach was how *Mark* went about it. In setting up his business hiring out luxurious portable loos for grand occasions, he viewed his family – including grandparents and brothers and uncles and aunts – as a source of free advice, information and other help.

One of the advantages of setting up at our age is that you can ask for help. I think a lot of relatives will be more willing to help than if you were, say, in your 40s. Certainly my grandparents and uncle and aunt expected to be approached for help.

Have you got any relatives in business who could give you some pointers or even some contacts? My uncle runs his own business in the flooring industry and he introduced me to his accountant. As my uncle has been a good client of the accountant for many years, he got me a very good deal. The accountant looks after the books and tax affairs for me, so I don't have to worry about these things and it doesn't cost me a fortune. That was thanks to my uncle.

If you follow a route most other people in your age group don't take – setting up your own business rather than getting a job – there are people other than your family who'll have a view on this: your friends.

When you're running your own business, you may find you mature faster than your mates, partly because you have greater responsibilities than they do. Your mate who works as a driver delivering parcels for a courier service only has his responsibilities as an employee, whereas you've got all the responsibilities of running a business. This aspect of starting up when you're 17 or 20 or 25 was emphasised by *Darren*, who is Mark's partner in the luxury loos business.

Even though Mark and I have only been in business two years, I think the gulf between me and my friends has grown. Having your own business matures you more quickly. Mark and I have had broader experiences than we'd have had in a job. We've met a variety of people and I've had to learn to interact with them and deal with them. When I worked as a driver for a courier firm, I just used to do the drop then leave. But now, one day I'm talking to a doctor, the next day I'm doing a sales presentation to a horse breeder.

Also I've had many varied experiences because in a small business, and especially in a growing business, I'm performing so many different functions. I'm not just a clerk in the office but I do spend some time on admin work in the office, nor am I just a driver, although I'm sometimes out on the road. I'm on the front line and I'm behind the scenes. In the morning I could be out leaflet dropping and in the afternoon dealing with the accountant. I'm changing activities during the day, not just driving a van all day. I certainly don't get bored! One of the advantages of running your own business is that you do lots of different things. Many of my friends feel bored much of the day because they do the same job day after day.

One thing I never read in any of the books or heard on the courses I've attended on how to set up and run a business is that, if your business is a success, you'll be the envy of some or all of your friends. Some of them will realise they are working and spending their days making money for someone else. But you probably won't know they are envious of your business being a growing success. I've come to realise that, when you're young, you are not particularly good at being happy for your peers, so don't expect to get compliments from your mates – quite the opposite, in fact. Both Mark and I have recently taken leases on BMWs and I'm surprised how many things my mates have been able to find about the car that they don't like!

These case histories help to bring out some of the particular obstacles you may face as a young person setting up and running your own business. Darren and Mark's idea for luxury portable loos met with considerable scepticism at first, even from the business counsellors they met. They also faced a number of obstacles, especially in raising the finance for what was seen to be a very risky enterprise. After all, how many people do you know who would want to rent a loo with real oil paintings for several hundred pounds a day? But they did their market research and became convinced that there were enough people and enough special occasions to make a sizeable market. And they were right. So we asked Darren and Mark to summarise some of the advantages and benefits of starting a business, and being your own boss, while you're young.

MARK: 'You can start building a future *for yourself* rather than build someone else's.'

DARREN: 'You can learn a lot more in life – and perhaps you learn faster by working for yourself when you're young.'

MARK: 'It can improve your relationship with your parents. They may like the fact you're "going for it" and showing you're willing to take on responsibility, in contrast to your mates who've simply drifted through school and then university because they didn't know what else to do.'

DARREN: 'Today, there's lots of help available for anyone who wants to set up a business, and there's even more assistance if you're under 20 or in your 20s, so take advantage of it. I went on a number of Business Link courses and the instructors told me that, by going on courses and learning the different aspects of starting a business, I had a much better chance of making a success of it.'

MARK: 'There's always the chance that you might hit upon something that turns out really well and grows and grows. If you'd like to earn really good money, you might come up with a business idea that does that.'

DARREN: 'Starting a business gives you the chance to spend your days doing something you love or enjoy rather than just going to work and getting a credit in your bank account once a month to pay the bills, hoping there's a bit left over for you to go out or put aside for your holiday. Don't just live for your weekends or for your holidays. I love getting in the orders for the business and I love seeing it grow and me and Mark have a laugh together – sometimes.'

MARK: 'With your own business you're not just earning income, you may be growing a "capital asset" for yourself; in other words, building up something that at a later date you could sell. We started our business from scratch, but we've now got corporate customers who come back to us regularly for the company do and we've built a reputation and a brand name. So already our accountant says we have a business that we could sell. Not that I want to.'

It's your business, it's your future.

CHAPTER 12
CUSTOMERS

We've already mentioned the help that's available from organisations such as Business Link and local enterprise agencies in setting up your business, and we're not going to duplicate that here. But there's still a lot to find out about, some of which can be picked up as you go along, so here and in the following chapters we'll focus on the information that others in your age group found most useful.

As you'd expect, anyone setting up a business needs to know the fundamentals. You might be asking: Do I need a licence to set up a business? What about tax? Can I start from home? But there are other matters that some young entrepreneurs found they had to grapple with that only came to light during the experience of actually setting up their business. For instance, many found it a real headache to price their product or service right.

As you work your way through the following chapters, you'll think of things you ought to do. Rather than rely on memory and risk the task getting overlooked, we suggest you make notes as you go along. In Appendix 4 we've provided an action checklist for you to use if you wish. You'll see that each task has a deadline by which time it should be completed!

Top of the list of questions for you to ask yourself about your new little business is: why should customers buy from me?

YOUR COURSE OF ACTION

When you set up in business, naturally you want it to be successful. But other people have the same ambition – your competitors.

So the question you face is: how do I induce potential customers to come to my business, rather to those competitors?

If we were to put that question to you, what would your response be? It's possible that you are one of a tiny – very fortunate – minority of people who set up in business blessed with having a product or service that is completely different from what others have got. Maybe you're an inventor and you've come up with something nobody else offers. Perhaps your name is Mr Dyson and you have come up with a revolutionary vacuum cleaner that will sweep away the competition. Or you've devised a product for which you can seek patent protection so the law will prevent others copying it. It would take years for others to find a way around your patent and put something on the market to compete with your product.

Or perhaps you're one of the overwhelming majority of people who set up in business without having a unique product or service.

Maybe your business idea is to open a garage that provides servicing and repairs of cars, or perhaps you're planning to sell fashion jewellery, or your business will hire out fancy dress costumes. It doesn't have the 'wow' factor: when you tell people your idea they don't raise their hands and say 'I wish I'd thought of that!' Your idea is one where you will be meeting commonplace needs and wants, for which there is plenty of demand – and therefore plenty of existing suppliers.

So, faced with the need to persuade potential customers to come to you rather than go to the competition, what will your response be? Many times we have put this question to would-be entrepreneurs about their fledgling businesses: how will you induce customers to come to you instead of to your competitors? Some of these young entrepreneurs talk about the quality of their product, others go into discussions about the level of service they will offer or, very often, they tell us they are going to be the cheapest.

One young guy – to save his embarrassment, we'll call him Barack – came to us about a year after he had set up his business. He told us he was struggling. His business involved a product – a high-ticket item that he sold to householders. When he launched his business, he'd told us: 'I'm going to do the best for my customers. I'm going to give them the best levels of service and I'm going to give them a really good price.' Now, one year down the line, he had this to report: 'As part of giving my customers the best level of service, I include a three-year warranty, on site, but I'm finding that the costs involved in this are such that I need to raise my price, but then I'd be a lot more expensive than a competitor in the same area. Or should I reduce my guarantee just to one year even though my competitor only offers a one-year guarantee and I wouldn't be any different from him.'

Barack is now doing something that, frankly, he should have done a year ago, before he set up the business. He is making a choice about the course of action he needs to take to stand out from the competition. If he had made that decision – and made the right choice – before he set up, he might not be struggling now. He had started to build a reputation and customers were beginning to understand what he stood for and what he offered – but he'd now got himself into a position where he had to change it.

Better to think *now* about the course of action you will take to stand out from the competition rather than leave it until a year after you've set up. That's not to say you won't ever change what you are doing in the light of experience. It's very likely that what works for a while has to be changed later, because the world around you changes. For instance, a new competitor comes into the market or an existing competitor changes what they are doing and it affects your business, or public opinion changes, or the government changes the law, or any one of a hundred other possibilities occurs that affects your business.

Barack's wish to do the best for his customers, to offer them the best price and the best level of service, seems laudable. But in trying to offer the best of everything, it may be that the business is spreading its efforts and its assets too thinly. His business – or perhaps your business if you took the same attitude – isn't seen by potential customers as standing for anything in particular; it's not *associated* with anything in particular. Take some highly successful household name companies and think for a few moments about what you associate with them. Suppose, for example, you wanted to buy a new TV. Go to the electrical store and you'll be faced with rows of televisions of different makes. If you wanted to buy a high-quality product, one that would last you several years, you might look at Sony televisions, because most consumers associate the Sony brand with high quality. But if you were on a limited budget and price was top of your priorities, you'd probably head for the display of a different brand.

No matter what trade or industry you are entering, there are a number of broad strategies open to you for making your business stand out from the competition; price and characteristics such as quality being only two of these. Below, we've included a list of five broad strategies that other young entrepreneurs have found useful (other business advisers might produce either a shorter or a longer list). We call this our PINCS list:

- **p**rice
- **i**nnovation
- **n**iche
- **c**haracteristics
- **s**ervice

Many of your predecessors in business have found it incredibly helpful to prioritise this list, to put one strategy at the top and then the others in descending order according to the role they will play in the business. In our experience, a lot of new small businesses have found that a workable approach is to take one particular broad strategy, put it at the top of the list, and make it paramount. Work really hard at that strategy, so that customers and potential customers associate you with it. That will mean customers looking for a high-quality product – if that's top of your list – will make a bee-line for you. Or if price is top of your list, you want customers to associate you with the best value. Customers seeking a discount product will head straight in your direction rather than going to see what the competition offers.

Earlier, in a different context, we pointed out a reality you have to face up to in setting up and running your own small business: that you have limited time. If, like Barack, you try to be all things to all people, you risk spreading your efforts too thinly. We have seen other small start-ups dilute their effort and get 'stuck in the middle', with low or very low profitability.

And there's something else we need to warn you about. If you try to offer the best of everything to everybody, you may end up unable to take the right decisions. We witnessed a young guy devise an interesting and innovative new product, but when he came to launch it on the market he priced it low in the hope of getting the biggest number of customers. But then competitors developed their own versions of that product and to keep up he had to spend money and time on changing his product to improve it. Sadly, the low margins that his low price gave him meant he didn't have enough resources to finance the research and development he needed.

PRICE

Perhaps selling at a low price will be your paramount strategy, so that customers who are looking for the best value will head straight to you. We'll be looking at how you can arrive at the right price for your product or service later, but for now here's a useful distinction to think about. It may be that the image you create is one of value for money, and that your marketing is such that customers will assume that by purchasing from you they will be getting the best value. But this is not necessarily the same as actually giving your customers the best value. Thanks to the Internet, it's easier than ever to compare prices, but there are still techniques open to you – and which are used by many successful businesses – to gently create the image that you are the leader when it comes to value for money. None of this involves any dishonest or illegal misrepresentations.

One of the commonest and biggest mistakes that new small businesses make is assuming that it's easy to sell things cheaply. It may be that, when you first set up, your overheads will be lower than the competition because you work from home or you don't employ other people. But as your business grows, so do your overheads and eventually your prices may have to go up too. But pushing up your prices can be hazardous: few customers like being on the receiving end of a price increase! Selling at low prices can be a strategy that's hard to sustain in the long term, so at least consider putting one of the other strategies at the top of your list.

INNOVATION

Maybe you could be a supplier of products who always has something new in your range or perhaps you have a product that you developed yourself, one that you can improve from time to time. Or a service that every so often offers something new. Darren and Mark, who hire out luxury portable loos, regularly add some new feature that they can talk about to hirers.

NICHE MARKETS

Not all business counsellors and business start-up books agree on a definition of 'niche' markets. We consider a niche market to be one where the needs of the buyers in that market are different from the needs of the average customer. As an example, let's take a business offering a cleaning service. This is a service that might be needed by all types of individuals, organisations and businesses; thus domestic households, offices and factories are routine customers. For these customers, the service provided by a typical contract-cleaning company would probably suffice. But that service wouldn't meet the needs of a hospital, which would require cleaning services of a higher than average standard, one that could cope with problems not met elsewhere. So a business that caters for the cleaning needs of hospitals is selling into a niche market.

So, could catering for a particular niche market be the factor that distinguishes your business from the competition?

CHARACTERISTICS

The quality of a product is one of its characteristics. We've already seen in Part One of this book that claiming your product is 'high quality' can mean a number of things. You might claim that your product is high quality because it performs better than the competition's or it's more durable. Or perhaps your business could build a reputation for product reliability.

These are all characteristics that could induce customers to purchase from you rather than from the competition. When deciding the characteristics of your product or service, don't overlook the fact that customers buy intangible benefits. To explain what we mean by intangible benefits, first we must point out that people 'buy' benefits: in other words, they buy what the product or service does for them.

Take spectacles, for instance. You pick up this mix of metal, glass, plastic and put it on your face, balancing it on your nose. Have you ever thought how dangerous that could be? Glass can be lethal, so why put it next to your eyes? If it breaks, the glass might blind the wearer! So why do it? You do it so you can see better, of course. That's what customers buy. The customer doesn't go into an optician's and say: 'Good morning – can I have a mix of metal, glass and plastic to balance on my nose?' What the customers buys is the benefit of being able to see better.

And that's how you must now view products. Ask yourself: what are the benefits that people are buying when they purchase a product? What does it do for them?

In the example of the spectacles, customers get the tangible benefit of being able to see better: they get a physical benefit. But people also buy intangible benefits. These are the psychological benefits that a product or service confers on the buyer. It may be, for example, that purchasing your product will give the buyer status. Or the buyer might take pride in owning your product. Or it might invoke some other pleasurable feeling in them such as a sense of nostalgia. These are all examples of benefits that could possibly distinguish your product from what the competition is offering and persuade customers to come to you.

SERVICE

Depending on the type of product or service you're offering, if you wish to make some aspect of service the factor that distinguishes you from the competition, you have a broad range of possibilities open to you.

It could be that you offer customers a wider choice than the competition, or that customers who come to you enjoy a level of expertise that the competition doesn't offer. Or your business might offer the best after-sales service or the highest level of stock so that customers could have what they want immediately. Or perhaps your business holds the largest stock of spare parts for the product.

YOU

In prioritising this list of options – if you choose to do this – and selecting the strategy you'll make your top priority, there's a key factor to take into account: your personality. In reality, if you want to maximise the success of your business, you don't have an absolutely free choice in deciding your paramount strategy. You can't just choose to make any of these strategies the one you work hardest at. As a small business, with you as the boss, you have to factor in your personality. Once again, we are asking you to take into account what would suit you. If your *Who Am I?* questionnaire has revealed that you are a creative individual, then perhaps you should consider innovation as your priority strategy. On the other hand, if you are selling on price, you'll probably need to be frugal to keep costs down and have a constant eye on the pounds and pence, but our experience of creative people is they often don't have the sort of personality suited to spending time poring over the accounts. They'd rather be writing, designing or working on a marketing campaign.

So which strategy would best suit your personality?

CHAPTER 13

BIRTH ANNOUNCEMENT

When you set up your business, not everyone will be a potential customer. Let's say you set up a business repairing and servicing washing machines and dishwashers. It's extremely unlikely that a 14-year-old boy or girl would be a customer for your services, but that's not to say that same 14-year-old is not a customer or potential customer for a different business. They might have a part-time job or a generous allowance from their parents and so have money to spend, which would make them potential customers for things like clothes, CDs and the cinema. It would be a waste of your time to attempt to sell your product or service to everybody, so identify who your potential customers are and direct your efforts at them.

Once you've worked out who your potential customers are, you have to cope with the fact that there will differences between them. Not all your potential customers are the same. Some of them, for example, may have red hair. Does that matter? Certainly not if your business is servicing and repairing washing machines and dishwashers, but if your product was hair colouring, then the original colour of the customer's hair would be relevant. So, having identified the potential customers for your product or service, your next task is to study the differences between them – the ones that matter to your business. And what matters to your business is the differences between customers that affect them when they come to make a purchase.

A classic example of this is age. The 14-year-old girl or boy who is almost certainly not a potential customer for a dishwasher-repair service could well be a potential customer for a mobile phone – and so might their 80-year-old grandmother. But the benefits that the 14-year-old wants from the mobile phone are very different from the benefits that the 80-year-old grandmother wants. Quite likely an 80-year-old is looking for something that is relatively simple to operate, partly because the more complex a product, the more likely it is to go wrong, and market research shows that older people prize reliability in a product. The 14-year-old will likely want lots of added features – an MP3 player, camera, radio, and so on. The 80-year-old grandmother probably wants a phone with big buttons that she can see easily.

These differences between the wants and needs of the 80-year-old and the 14-year-old apply across a whole range of other products for which they might both be potential customers. The really important factor to remember is that if you try to offer a product or service you think might suit every potential customer, then you could end up with something that doesn't really satisfy the needs or wants of anyone.

We saw in the previous chapter the danger of your spreading your time and effort too thinly when it comes to trying to induce customers to come to *your* business rather than to the competition. This is especially relevant to a new small business, where you have limited resources, including a limited amount of time for each of the functions you have to carry out. Likewise, there's the same danger when it comes to working out what will please potential customers. If you try to devise a business with a product or service that suits every type of potential customer, you may end up missing out. It might be to your advantage to concentrate on just some of the potential buyers rather than spread your efforts thinly.

The age of the customer is likely to affect their choice of product or service: an 18-year-old will have very different needs from someone who's 48 or even 68. Rather than getting to grips with everyone's needs, your limited time might be better spent on trying to understand the needs and wants of what the marketing professionals call a 'market segment' – buyers who share a characteristic that influences their choice of product or service. The closer you can get to understanding what one group of buyers is looking for, the more likely it is that you'll be able to please them.

When you first set up your business, the temptation to try and reel in every potential customer that's out there is understandable, because you need the income. This might be hard for you to accept, but it could be better to spend your time concentrating on attracting just one segment of potential buyers. It's not easy to turn your back at this stage on what you think might be potential customers, but by devising a product or service that, as far as possible, meets the needs of what a group of buyers is looking for, you could end up with more buyers than if you'd offered a mish-mash that didn't really suit anybody.

Write here in the box who you see as your potential customers:

SPREAD THE WORD

Take an A4 sheet of paper – or a bigger sheet, such as a sheet of flip-chart paper if you've got one – and write on it the following:

I CAN'T BUY FROM YOU
BECAUSE I DON'T KNOW
YOU EXIST

Fill up the whole sheet with this sentence. Write it in capital letters. In red ink. Then pin it up somewhere where you will see it every day while you're setting up and launching your business.

You haven't got a business until you've got customers. So the world has to know that you are open for business.

One of the authors is a keen young sportsman; the other isn't. But even this older one who isn't interested in sport occasionally catches a little of it on the TV, usually while waiting for another programme to start. And what catches his eye is not what the players or competitors are doing, but the brand names on what they are wearing and that are displayed around the ground or the arena or the track – names we're all familiar with such as Samsung, Vodafone, Canon, Virgin or Dell. These brands are famous the world over and have probably been known to you for years, but the companies behind these famous brand names know it's essential to keep those names in the public eye. So if it's necessary for famous names with which we are familiar to keep reminding us of their existence, how crucial is it for your business to let the world know you're here?

The good news is that, depending on the type of business you have, and whether you are selling to the public or to other businesses, there are a number of ways in which you can promote your business either at no cost or low cost. And more good news is that, in our experience, once you get those first orders in and get the ball rolling, you start to gain momentum and other orders can follow those early ones. We'll show you how and why this can happen later in this chapter.

TELL THE WORLD

We do literally mean *tell* people: speak to people. Take every opportunity to tell people about your product or service. Tell everybody you can – it's free advertising!

Tell your relatives, tell your neighbours, tell your mates. Contact people you don't see very often and tell them. And enlist the help of others to spread the message – get your mum and dad, your sister or brother and your aunt and uncle to tell people. Consider arming these helpers with a leaflet they can pass on, but don't just give them one leaflet – give them a supply.

And here's a tip: don't make the mistake of only telling people you think might be a potential customer for your product or service. Tell everybody! Because the person who isn't a potential customer might mention it to somebody who *is*.

REFERRALS

Here's another method of getting customers that won't cost you anything. Ask people to help you by giving you referrals. These are names and contact details of other people they can suggest who might be interested in hearing what you have to offer. So go to Auntie Mary and Uncle Jack, tell them about your exciting new business, find out if they're interested in becoming a customer, thereby helping you to get started, and then ask them if they can suggest other people who might be interested.

Another tip: don't just ask for 'some' names and addresses. Give them a specific number of names to hand over. How many names you ask for will depend on the type of product or service. If it's a specialised purchase, it might be unrealistic to expect Auntie Mary or Uncle Jack to give you a list of 20 potential customers. But it might not be unrealistic if what you are supplying is a common or even everyday purchase.

RECOMMENDATIONS

We said earlier that once you get those first few orders, you may find you gain some momentum and that other orders then start to come in. And here's a reason why: you will – of course – have very satisfied customers. We hope you will have *delighted* customers. If you supply customers with what they expect to receive, then they will be – or should be – satisfied. If you give them less than they were led to believe they'd receive, they'll be disappointed. Provide *more* than they expect and they may be delighted. Both satisfied and delighted customers may provide you with repeat orders *and* also recommend you to others. Naturally, customers who are delighted, rather than just satisfied, are more likely to recommend you.

If you are fortunate enough to have a product that is visual, the more likely it is that you'll receive recommendations. For example, when Barrie set up his business supplying made-to-measure loose covers for sofas, he quickly found that a good percentage of customers came from recommendations. This was because the product was very visual. The next door neighbour, seeing the sofa or suite with its new covers, might make the mistake of thinking this was new furniture. The customer would reveal that it was the old tatty suite made to look new by these new loose covers. So both the neighbour and other people visiting the house have seen Barrie's product and been impressed by the transformation. It was no surprise, then, that some of the callers at the house would ask who had supplied this lovely product.

But don't just rely on the goodwill of satisfied customers; you can help the process along. Here are two techniques you can use to boost the number of recommendations. One is to get in the habit of *asking* your customers to recommend you. Say to them something along the lines that if they're happy with the product or service, would they be kind enough to tell others. Explain that yours is a new small business and that you don't have the funds to pay for advertising in glossy magazines. Add that one of the reasons your pricing is so competitive is because you *don't* spend a fortune on advertisements.

You can further encourage customers to recommend you by rewarding them for doing so. With Barrie's furniture covers business, he would tell customers that if they were kind enough to recommend his business and it resulted in an order, he would give the customer who'd done the recommending a gift. In his case, the gift was some loose cushions which matched the suite. As Barrie bought these at trade price, this was a very inexpensive way of getting more custom. And yet the recommending customer was delighted to receive something so presentable. Also, when a customer has recommended you, it's probably going to be easier than usual to make a sale to the person whose name has been passed on. This is a win-win situation for the business.

So, aim to have delighted customers and also put in place a recommend-a-friend scheme. Draft a leaflet that you can print off at home on your inexpensive ink-jet printer and leave this with the customer. Include in the leaflet a picture of the gift they will receive if their recommendation is successful and a coupon for them to fill in the name and address of the friend/relative/neighbour who might be interested in your product or service. Also include a space for satisfied customers to comment on your product or service. Ask them if you can use this comment on your website or in your brochure.

DROP LEAFLETS

Door-to-door leaflets, or drop leaflets as they are also called, can be an economical way of telling the world about your product or service and acquiring new customers – especially if you are prepared to do the legwork yourself.

We're not suggesting you print ten thousand leaflets on your ink-jet printer at home; local professional printers will often give you an extremely competitive price for a single-colour drop leaflet. The more you buy, the cheaper they get. Adam, who set up an American-style ice-cream parlour, announced its opening by pushing a leaflet through the letterboxes of ten thousand homes locally, and the printing cost for this quantity of A5 size single colour leaflets was just £65 from a one-person local printing service.

Drop leaflets can have advantages other than their modest cost. With Barrie's loose covers business, he had two or three attempts at different wording. Once he'd found the text that was most effective at producing inquiries, he was then in a position to know that if he put out a certain number of leaflets this would produce a particular number of orders. Apart from those times of the year when trade was traditionally quiet, such as the peak holiday period of August and just after Christmas when customers' bank accounts were depleted, the drop leaflets provided a steady source of custom.

AN AUDIENCE

Earlier in the chapter we urged you to talk to people, to tell them that you are open for business. But you shouldn't confine this to talking to individuals: your product or service may be one where you could find an audience to address.

Lee and his family were fortunate to live in a part of the UK where crime rates, including burglaries, were low. But as unemployment in the region rose, so too did crime levels. Lee set up a burglar alarm company which offered a system designed especially for the home. His market research had convinced him that, although shops, warehouses and other business premises were obvious potential customers for alarms, there were already several established suppliers. Lee felt that by specialising in a burglar alarm system for the home he had more chance of getting a place in the market than if he tried to cater for every type of customer.

He also felt it might be a product that lent itself to raising leads (enquiries) by drop leaflets. He decided to scan the local newspapers – the paid-for paper and the free one – for reports of burglaries. While the news of a burglary was fresh in the mind of local residents he, with the help of his young brother, would deliver leaflets in the locality where the burglary had taken place. This did produce some business, but Lee also needed other ways to reach potential customers.

His mum suggested he give a talk to the local over-60s club, not just about burglar alarms but about security in general. Lee was pleasantly surprised one evening to find himself facing a group of some 50 people who were interested in learning about such matters as personal security and, of course, security in the home. Lee gave each member of the audience a leaflet offering a free, no-obligation security check of homes and a no-obligation demonstration of how simple his system was to operate.

Don't tell us you'd be too nervous to speak to a group! You probably did presentations at school or uni and you could have a rehearsal in front of some of the family or some friends.

BE YOUR OWN REPORTER

Research shows that when we read advertisements in newspapers and magazines we do so with a degree of scepticism, as you might expect, but that we have a different attitude towards news reports or features. Therefore, if you could get a news item or feature about your business into the press, it could be a very effective way of letting potential customers know that your business exists.

Naturally, newspapers and magazines are wary of attempts by businesses to manufacture news. But if you have something of genuine newsworthy interest to readers, grab pen and paper, or sit down at the computer, and draft a press release.

The launch of your business – a new enterprise in the area – is a genuine piece of news that's of interest to local residents. And starting a business at your young age offers a different angle. Editors like to add visual interest to their pages with photos, so you could bump up your chances of getting a feature in the local paper by holding an opening ceremony and inviting some well-known local personality. Ring the newspaper a few days beforehand and tell them about this so that they can send a photographer to capture the event. If yours is an e-business, try to avoid the usual photo of just you at the computer – include in the photo something visual connected with what you are offering.

After the initial opening of your business, from time to time you could submit a press release about some newsworthy development or event. This might be about your business presenting a prize to the winner of a competition you held for customers. Or your fledgling business has just signed up customer number 500. Or your business has grown and you are now moving into premises which will enable you to offer an even better service to customers.

Here's the right approach to drafting a press release – remember that reporters are busy people and the less work they have to do in making your copy ready for press, the more likely it is they will accept it.

Type your press release using double line spacing and leave wide margins. Read the newspaper or magazine you are targeting and try to copy their style. How long are the sentences and paragraphs? You could e-mail or post your press release to the editor, although an editor advised us: 'With an e-mail it's all too easy to click on "delete". A hard copy document seems more substantial.' And check out the last date for submitting items to the publication, especially with monthlies like the glossy county journals – miss the date and it could be old news for the next edition.

A final tip: make sure your press release is about something readers will find interesting and that's genuinely newsworthy – editors won't want to simply publish a plug for your product or service. If you want that, they'll expect you to pay for an advertisement!

WWW.MYWEBSITE

We've suggested several ways for you to publicise your business and reach potential customers that will involve you in either no expenditure or make only a small dent in your budget. There are of course other channels, including paid-for advertising, mailshots and, with the aid of today's technology, via your own website and e-mail and via networking websites.

Most people who have an e-mail account will almost certainly have some provision for identifying or barring 'spam'. This and the enormous quantities of spam – including foreign e-mails received – can be a huge bar to the effectiveness of this way of reaching potential customers.

Consider joining Facebook, if you haven't already. It's a way of spreading the word, telling people you're setting up and what you will be doing. Ask your friends on Facebook to tell their friends and spread the word for you. Look at joining other networking groups. The LiveWIRE programme for young entrepreneurs, funded by Shell, offers free information and advice, so promote yourself and your business on the website (**www.shell-livewire.org**).

For many businesses today, a web presence is almost essential, but it will of course involve you in some expenditure. Even if you don't intend to make sales of your product via the web, many potential customers today will nevertheless expect a business to have a website they can visit to learn more about the product or service being offered.

Your website will have to be designed and it will need hosting. Some providers of hosting services offer build-your-own website kits to enable you to do this yourself at no cost. Whether or not this would be sufficient to impress customers depends to some extent on how professional your business needs to look. Your self-build website might be good enough if you are offering a part-time, dog-walking service to a local community. A professionally designed website is likely to cost from a few hundred pounds upwards.

You can find lots of useful tips about promoting your business online in the book *Virtually Free Marketing* by Philip R. Holden, listed in Appendix 3.

How will you make potential customers aware of you? Make some notes here:

CHAPTER 14
THE PRICE IS RIGHT

Earlier in the book, the term 'market research' crept in. We didn't make a fuss of it then because, frankly, a lot of young, would-be entrepreneurs find the term off-putting. Perhaps it's the word 'research' that does it. Maybe you think 'research' is something that academics do and it would involve you in masses of writing.

But market research can be enjoyable and, in any case, it's essential that you do it. And you should do it before you actually launch your business, as it will help you to discover whether the idea is viable, if there are customers out there and what they will pay, among other things. Famous-name, highly successful companies put a huge amount of effort into market research. If Toyota, Cadbury, Nokia or Nike find they need to do it, surely you ought to follow their example? It's not difficult – you can do it yourself – and the benefits you might gain will far outweigh the effort you put in.

The sort of things you need to find out about include:

■ existing and potential customers;

■ what products or services are out there now; and

■ who is supplying these products or services.

CUSTOMERS

You could devise a simple questionnaire and go out and talk to prospective customers face to face or e-mail or post the questionnaire to them. If your customers are likely to be spread throughout the UK, face-to-face research is clearly going to be time-consuming or costly, but if you are able do it, it has the advantage that you can easily put supplementary questions to the interviewee in response to their answers.

Let's suppose you are considering setting up a pizza delivery service in your local area. You might want to know the following information from local residents.

1. **Do you eat pizza?**

2. **If not, why not?**

3. **Do you use a pizza delivery service?**

4. If not, why not?

5. If you use a delivery service, how often do you use the service?

6. How could your current delivery service be improved (e.g. better containers, faster delivery time)?

7. How much do you usually spend?

8. How do you feel about the price?

9. Would you pay more for the improvements suggested in question 6 and, if so, how much?

One prospective entrepreneur who was contemplating setting up a pizza delivery service carried out market research along the lines we suggested. In his locality he discovered that most users of the existing service were dissatisfied with the waiting times, especially on Thursday, Friday and Saturday evenings. He cut the waiting time and sent the competition reeling by coming up with this solution: cooking the pizza in the van on the way to the delivery. By doing his market research, talking to buyers, he became convinced there was room in the market for him if he could overcome the most common complaint. His research also convinced him that long waiting times was such a deterrent that it put customers off ordering and that cutting waiting times would increase demand.

He also discovered that a percentage of potential customers did not know there was a pizza delivery service operating in their area. This showed that the existing provider was failing to make its existence known to customers: their advertising and public relations were not working effectively. If a new business were now to investigate how the existing provider was publicising their service, it could then improve upon these methods.

Here, you're carrying out your own original market research, but you can also use the research that others have done. You can find much of this from the Internet or at the local reference library. Market research companies, publishers of trade magazines, universities, trade associations and other bodies produce reports and studies, most of which are freely available. You can uncover valuable and interesting info about the size of the market you are thinking of entering, as well as current trends, what products are available, pricing, and much else.

As soon as you have your first customers you have your own unique source of information. Once you are making sales, it doesn't mean you shouldn't still be thinking of ways to improve your product or service or devise new ones or find new markets to go into. So talk to your customers. Try to find out what they liked about your product or service and what other products or services they might be interested in buying.

Carrying out market research makes it a safer risk to set up in business; it's also the more intelligent way to go about it. And just because your business will be small, it doesn't mean you can get away with setting it up in an amateurish way.

THE COMPETITION

We mentioned earlier that your market research should include finding out who the existing suppliers are for the product or service you have in mind: your future competitors. You can learn a great deal from them, as we saw earlier, such as how they may be failing to tell potential customers that they're alive.

Yet, incredibly, some people who set up in business fail to find out who and what it is that they will be going up against. And a few of these fledgling entrepreneurs decide – amazingly – that they don't *want* to find out. They deliberately close their eyes so they won't see the competition. Such behaviour is an enormous puzzle to us. One girl we knew of had done quite a bit of market research but when we asked her about the competition she said: 'I don't want to know!' We shook our heads in wonder. Why not? 'Because I so love my idea and it would be so disappointing to find that somebody else is already doing it,' she told us.

This is an example of one of the dangers you face if you are too much in love with a particular business idea. Just as love can make you blind to your boyfriend or girlfriend's failings, so too it can blind you to the shortcomings of your business idea. If you have a strong competitor, or too many competitors, your little business might struggle to survive.

So we said to this girl: you *do* want to know if somebody else is already doing this. Better to find out now before you start, than after you've launched. Our advice to you is: become an expert. Become an expert on the competition.

A useful approach to take is to put yourself in the shoes of a prospective customer for the product or service. How would they go about finding out who the suppliers are? Do what they would do: look online, flick through Yellow Pages and look at the adverts in the local paper. Study the suppliers' advertising, read their leaflets thoroughly and evaluate their websites. You might be able to see and handle the product or service or even try it out. Or you could pose as a potential customer and ask for a sales presentation.

As soon as you start this process of putting yourself in the position of a potential customer, you start the learning process. Right at the beginning you will find out how easy or difficult it is to get to know what the supplier offers. When you contact them, how do they deal with enquiries? Do they strike you as efficient? If you really were a customer for this product or service, do you think you would be happy to place an order with this supplier?

CASE STUDY

Lee, who set up a burglar alarm company specialising in alarms for the home, was persuaded to pose as a prospective customer of what would be his main competitor. This was a local firm who had been established for some 30 years and supplied alarms to both households and businesses. But most of their work came from business clients and Lee wondered if they had the right approach when it came to dealing with householders.

The sales representative who came to give him a quotation for installing an alarm was an ex-police officer. It became clear from his visit that he was more concerned with the technological and security aspects than with making a sales presentation. A lot of what he told Lee was very technical and some of it Lee couldn't understand.

In the light of this, Lee decided that, as he wanted to concentrate solely on selling to householders, he would try to make his sales presentation livelier, more interesting and easier to understand. In particular he would take along a working sample of his product and involve the potential customer in a demonstration of how the alarm worked. This proved to be very effective, as his system worked by detecting movement. 'Sit still in your chair and the system won't detect you,' he would say to the prospective customer. He'd then ask them to stand up: a warning light would immediately flash to show that the system had detected this movement. He did of course switch off the external sounder beforehand in case the sudden noise gave his prospective customer a heart attack!

The demonstration also proved to the customer how simple the system was to operate, as they didn't need the complications of a system designed to secure high-risk commercial premises. And the potential customer could see the attractive unit, in which the workings were housed, and which was designed especially for the home environment.

Having been on the receiving end of a visit and presentation by his future competitor, Lee was able to come up with a number of ways in which to improve the presentation.

Here are four boxes in which we ask you to set down your summary of what you have found out about the competition.

Who are your competitors?

What are their strengths?

What are their weaknesses?

How will you stand out from the competition?

A QUESTION OF PRICE

Top of your list of what you need to discover about the competition is: what's their price?

In our experience, many people setting up a business find this the most difficult question of all to answer: what price shall I sell my product or service at?

We pointed out earlier that many would-be entrepreneurs coming into business for the first time mistakenly assume that the fast and easy route to business success is to sell cheaper than everybody else. Let's remind you of some of the dangers inherent in this assumption. Firstly, while it may be possible to sell cheaply at the outset, it is often difficult to maintain a low-price strategy in the longer term. Secondly, many big successful suppliers create the impression customers should go to them for the best price, and they buy in such bulk that they have the benefit of profit margins you won't have. Thirdly, with some products it is difficult to evaluate their worth – jewellery, for example – and many customers will take the view that a low price must mean low quality: do you want to be perceived as selling a low-quality product?

This question of perception is even more of a problem when it comes to services. If the quote you give for the provision of a service is the lowest quote, will the customer expect you to deliver the worst service? When it comes to services, many customers, whether buying for themselves or buying for business, often get three quotations and accept the one in the middle. This way, they think they are avoiding being 'ripped off' by paying too much but also avoiding getting the cheapest, most inferior service.

Please pause here and reflect on what we are about to tell you: it's vital. Get the price wrong and you will have no business.

We've seen newly launched businesses that appear to be very successful in the early stages. This impression is created by a business having lots of customers and lots of turnover. In other words people were spending money with the business. But because the price was wrong, it didn't give that business enough margin to cover its costs. On the other hand, of course, if you set your price too high you may find you don't have enough customers and so you still don't cover your costs. (We're not saying that you should never consider setting a very high price for your product or service: it could indicate that the product or service was of very high quality, provided there is sufficient demand for such quality product at a high price.) Pricing *can* be a simple matter but in many instances it will require much research and much thought. Often the most successful businesses are those which are clever at pricing.

Many newcomers to business take the following simplistic approach to arriving at the price at which they will offer their product or service. They look at what the cost will be to them and then add on an arbitrarily selected percentage. Sometimes the percentage they add on is one which simply appears to them to sound reasonable. We've heard people say things such as: 'I am going to add on 25 per cent. I'm not greedy, I think that sounds reasonable.' This simplistic approach overlooks the fact that what may be an appropriate margin for one type of product may be completely inappropriate for another. For example, if you are selling a product for which there is a repeat demand, you may be able to work on a lower margin. In contrast, if the purchase is an occasional one and your sales fewer, you will probably need to work on a much higher margin.

We've seen some newcomers to business recoil in horror when they discover what might be the accepted margin to add on in some particular trades. Take jewellery as an example. Compare how often people buy a ring with how often they buy a loaf of bread. If you were to set up in business retailing inexpensive fashion jewellery, you would likely find that your wholesale suppliers recommend you mark up the jewellery to retail for at least two or three times what you paid for it wholesale. A jewellery stall on the Saturday crafts and gifts market might make only 30 or 40 sales in one day at an average retail price of say £4 per item. We'll be looking later at how to work out your business costs, but for now we can see that the business must have margins wide enough to cover stall rent and other outgoings such as petrol and telephone. If the average buying-in price for each item of jewellery were £1 and the proprietor added on only 25 per cent and retailed at £1.25, she would almost certainly pack up within a few weeks. But by retailing at an average of three times cost, it may be that – depending on the proprietor's goals for the business – the day's trading was profitable.

WHAT SHALL I CHARGE FOR MY SERVICE?

If your business is one providing a service rather than selling a product, then there are particular considerations to take into account.

You might come up against this obstacle: the customer's narrow view of how you should price your services. They often think you should price a service according to how many hours' work you'll be putting in – and they may have definite views on what you should be paying yourself per hour. You, in working out what you will charge for your services, will quite properly take account of the degree of skill involved and how much experience you bring to the job. However, when you set up in a service business you may find the large number of competitors you're up against is a problem. This is because very often the set-up costs for a service-based business are low. Set up a service providing garden maintenance and you could find yourself in competition against two or three single-person businesses who advertise on the board in the local newsagent's. Those newsagent-board advertisers may be happy to charge a low hourly rate for a number of reasons, including the fact they've been able to set up in business by purchasing a second-hand lawn mower and a few garden tools – not much outlay there. Or they might be doing it part-time and merely supplementing their pension.

With a service business you'll also find that customers have their own perception about the value of the benefit they'll receive from the service. We've all heard stories about the high rates some plumbers charge for an emergency call-out, but put yourself in the position of the customer. It's late at night in December, a bitterly cold night, you're a pensioner living alone and the central heating has gone off, you have no other form of heating…you will be very grateful for that plumber who turns out. After all, you are receiving very considerable benefit from the work they will perform. You will place a much higher value on their labour than you will on the services of the jobbing gardener who weeds the flower border on a sunny afternoon in summer. So, in working out the price at which you will offer your service, you need to take into account the likely value that costumers will place on the service, which is formed by the degree of benefit they consider themselves to be receiving.

One of the ways in which you can boost the perceived value that customers receive is to enhance your status as the provider.

When co-author Luke set up his business as a fitness trainer we included his qualification in his advertising sales literature and on his business cards. Luke's professional qualifications in fitness training and nutrition gave customers increased confidence that they could rely on his service. For this element of security customers expect to pay a higher rate.

There's another – perhaps surprising – reason why customers might be prepared to pay more for some services. A percentage of customers are likely to pay a higher rate if they've seen your picture in the local paper or heard you speak on the radio! Being a well-known provider of a service seems, in some customers' eyes, to confer a degree of status upon you – and the higher your status, the higher the rate you may be able to charge. So, when a news item breaks in the national newspapers or on the television news, such as the findings of some new fitness research, Luke contacts his local radio station, to let them know he's available for interviews where he could comment on – and add to – the new findings, based on his own experience. If nothing else, existing clients may be pleased to hear their fitness trainer on the radio, as he's clearly an expert whose views are sought by others. That existing client might tell a friend – who then signs up with this well-known fitness trainer.

If you enjoyed writing essays at school or college, how about moving on to writing articles? You could write a piece about your particular subject for the local paper or even a national magazine. It would help you to get known, and perhaps bring in customers, and also enhance your status and therefore the rates you could charge for your service. One of our local newspapers regularly features an article written by a solicitor on some legal issue, complete with a picture of his friendly face. OK, you might not be a lawyer, but if you were setting up a part-time dog-walking service you could write a short article on some useful aspect of looking after a dog. As with a press release, you should write in the same style as the newspaper or magazine but, unlike with a press release, you might be paid for the article. You could even be asked to write for the publication on a regular basis. The result? Free publicity and an additional source of income!

ADDING VALUE

You could add value to your product or service by including some extra element that would allow you to charge a higher price than the competition. So you might come up with something that increased your costs by, say, five per cent, but which enabled you to increase your price by 10 per cent. We can see that packaging adds value for certain types of product. For instance, we, as customers, often pay more for a bodycare product because the item comes in lavish packaging, which, in our eyes, enhances its status. Chocolate is another example: we'll pay more for an attractive box that turns the chocolates into a very presentable gift. If you are offering a service, maybe it could come with a guarantee? At your sales presentation, you could produce a guarantee certificate, printed in a fancy typeface complete with scrolls? Surely a service which comes with such documented guarantee is worth more than one which does not provide the security of a certificate for the customer to retain? The certificate might have cost you just 10p to produce on your ink-jet printer.

THE PRESENTATION OF PRICE

Nearly as important as getting the price right is how you present the price to the customer. Whether or not you achieve a sale could depend on the manner in which you convey the price to the customer. With many types of product, the biggest objection the prospective customer will raise is the price – it's too high. But there are a number of techniques you can use to present the price in a good light.

One technique commonly used by professional salespeople is to build up the customer's expectations of the price. In other words, they lead the customer to expect the price, when revealed, to be higher than it actually is.

CASE STUDY

Meena set up a business working from home, making and supplying made-to-measure curtains. She aimed for upmarket customers in big houses who wanted grand curtains for their big rooms, complete with all the trimmings. She was surprised to find that high-income customers were not necessarily unconcerned about price – quite often, the opposite in fact. Her dad had been a professional salesman before taking early retirement and gave Meena some useful professional tips on how to go about revealing to customers what the price would be. One tactic was to take time in working out the price for the customer and not to rush it. It was necessary for Meena to take a considerable number of measurements and, in doing this properly, it helped to convey to the customer how much work would be involved in making up the curtains.

You can't use this approach if there's a standard price for the job or product, but it's a technique that's particularly suited to jobs involving labour, where the price has to be individually calculated. If this applies to your product, then try to make sure the customer sees you jotting down the figures, drawing your rough diagrams and punching away on your calculator. It may be that the actual price then comes as a pleasant surprise. Another tactic used by professional salespeople when quoting the price is to break it down into various components, rather than giving a straightforward price for the whole job. It will help to make the price seem more reasonable if you itemise what the customer is getting and if you go through it with the customer to show them how the price is built up.

Let's round off this chapter with one final – very nice – thought about pricing. There are some customers out there waiting for you who want a really high price. The price tells them that this is an exclusive product that most other people can't afford and it demonstrates to their friends and acquaintances and neighbours how well-off they are!

CHAPTER 15
GET THAT SALE

When you're in business, you're in the business of selling. So please don't say to us: I'm not a salesperson. We're *all* salespeople. You're selling yourself when you chat up a boy/girl for a date. You sell yourself at a job interview. So why not improve your ability as a salesperson by making sure you're familiar with at least the fundamental techniques of selling. Let's give you an example of the sort of basic error that is often made and which you can avoid.

A potential customer goes into a store and begins to browse. Mr Amateur Salesperson approaches her and says: 'Can I help you?' Sounds helpful, doesn't it? But it's not helpful to the sales process. It's requiring the customer to give a yes or no answer.

And what a difficult choice: if they say 'yes' then they're committing themselves to something, even if it's only some sales talk, but perhaps at this stage all they want to do is look around. On the other hand, if they respond with 'no' then they've rebuffed the assistant and pretty much stopped the exchange stone dead. Good salespeople recognise the psychological factors at work in the sales process. In this example, it would be better to have simply engaged the customer in conversation. Perhaps the salesperson could have made some comment about the item the customer was looking at, briefly telling the customer something that might interest them. Such as: 'We do have that in other colours as well' or 'We have that item in bigger and smaller sizes, if that isn't the right size'. Backed up with a friendly smile.

Let's remind ourselves here what it is that people buy. They buy *benefits*. They buy what the product or service will do for them. The benefit that customers get from their purchase can be either a physical benefit and/or a psychological one. Food in your stomach satisfies your need for nutrition, and the surroundings of the restaurant in which you consume your food may put you in a relaxed frame of mind. As a customer of that restaurant you are getting both physical and psychological benefits from your purchase. Psychological benefits include pride in ownership – owning the product enhances your status – and reinforcement of your sense of individuality. The purchaser of a BMW might take pride in the excellence of its engineering; the owner of a Breitling watch might enjoy being on the receiving end of envious glances from friends when they spot it on his or her wrist; someone in a tailor-made suit takes pleasure in wearing clothes that have been made especially for them, incorporating the features they want, rather than making do with whatever features the off-the-peg suit comes with.

YOU

Nick, who set up a sales training business, opens his courses by reminding the trainee salespeople that, when attempting to make a sale, they are in fact selling two things: 'You have to sell yourself to the customer and you have to sell your product to the customer.' This is especially true when selling services. A customer relies on the people they are buying from to do the job they've promised to do, and to do it properly. So the builder or the decorator or the driveway contractor who comes to give you a quote will be making it harder for themselves if you are put off by their appearance or their manner. So, if you're considering setting up as a supplier of services involving manual work, it doesn't mean you are entitled to turn up dressed slovenly. Barrie recalls a fencing contractor who came to give him a quote and thought it was OK to throw in a few swearwords; he didn't get the order. Luke has been on the receiving end of sales assistants who, he felt, treated him with an air of contempt because he was young. As a young person yourself, it's unlikely you'd be guilty of the latter – but would you fall into the trap of not being as polite as you should be to an elderly person who's taking a long time to count out the right money?

Be polite, not pushy, and you've already done a lot towards getting the customer to form a favourable view of you. Add in a helpful manner and demonstrate that you are listening to what the customer says and the customer will be well on their way to trusting you – and perhaps taking your advice and your suggestions.

If all this seems obvious to you, pause and reflect for a moment on how often you have come up against examples of salespeople who don't seem to know how to deal with customers. Or don't care. Have you ever stood at a sales counter, feeling like a lemon, while a couple of assistants chat to themselves, ignoring you?

Many salespeople present an image that is too abrasive; others like to cultivate the image of a high-flying executive, which might be appropriate if your prospective customers are themselves affluent executives, but probably unsuitable for many face-to-face situations. When selling to the general public, it might be best to avoid the expensive executive briefcase and other such accoutrements.

As a salesperson, whether selling a product or service, you will of course be very pleased to get repeat orders and recommendations. You can hope to get these if you've given your customers what they expected to get – and you can hope to get many more of them if what you have provided has delighted your customers. But you can wave goodbye to the prospect of repeat orders and/or recommendations if you have a disappointed customer. And that brings us to the question of customer service.

CUSTOMER SERVICE

Even if your business is one that provides a product rather than delivers a service, it will still have a service element. For example, will you deliver the product on time? How will you deal with complaints if the product isn't up to standard? Good-quality customer service is so important to businesses today that many employees are sent on customer service training courses. You can start your own customer service training by thinking of bad examples of service you've received as a customer. Analyse what was wrong. Draw up a list of these in the box below – they are examples of what you will not do to customers in your business.

Here are some examples of poor customer service. You won't do any of the following, will you?

■ Fail to turn up to an appointment without any explanation.

■ Turn up late without calling beforehand to say you will be late, apologising and giving the reason.

■ Fail to turn up on the appointed day and then simply turn up out of the blue on another day.

■ Send different goods from those which were ordered without clearing this with the customer beforehand.

■ Sound bored when a customer talks to you.

■ Fail to write or phone or e-mail to let the customer know the goods will be delayed and to explain why.

■ Talk to a customer in a manner in which you would not want to be spoken to, just because of the way they dress or their accent.

And here are some things *not* to say to customers in the course of your business.

■ 'I've no idea when I'll be there, mate.'

■ 'We don't do that – we shouldn't have said that we could.'

■ 'Yes, dear?'

■ 'No, we changed our opening hours – I forgot to tell you.'

The sales process involves much more than what goes on at the stage where a sale is about to be clinched. It begins with the initial enquiry. How well was the telephone enquiry dealt with? Was the e-mail enquiry promptly replied to?

Here's a word-for-word transcript of a telephone conversation one of the authors endured when trying to find a supplier for a summerhouse.

TELEPHONE RINGS ELEVEN TIMES BEFORE IT IS ANSWERED.

Homer: Hello.

Me: Hello?

Homer: Hello.

Me: Is that Homer's Sectional Buildings?

Homer: Yes.

Me: Good morning.

SILENCE

Me: I was wondering if you are open today.

Homer: Well, obviously or I wouldn't be here to answer the phone.

SURPRISED SILENCE AT MY END.

Me: Can you tell me what time you close please?

Homer: We are open until round about lunchtime.

Me: Well, can you be a bit more precise. What's round about lunchtime mean?

Homer: If we only have a few customers we shut.

PAUSE

Me: Well how am I supposed to know whether you are open or not – it's a half-hour journey for me to come to you?

Homer: It's underneath the counter.

Me: Sorry?

Homer: I was talking to somebody else.

LOUD CRASHING NOISE. APPARENTLY HOMER WAS DOING SOMETHING ELSE AS WELL AS TALKING TO SOMEBODY ELSE AND TO ME, A CUSTOMER, AND HE HAD DROPPED AN OBJECT.

At that point we were cut off. You might find it useful to re-read this script and make a list in the box of the failings shown by the person who was representing the business on the phone.

Unfortunately, not all customers know how to conduct themselves either. A tiny percentage – perhaps two per cent – are unreasonable, and a microscopic percentage, perhaps 0.002 per cent, are crazy. Probably you will need to have been in business for a while to learn to spot early the signs given out by a customer who is going to be too much aggravation to deal with, but if you do spot them, then politely and quickly withdraw. Why should you put up with the arrogant customer who treats you with contempt? You don't need their money *that* much and putting up with it only encourages such behaviour.

USE YOUR EARS

Even today, the common perception of a professional salesperson is of a fast-talking individual pressurising the customer into buying something they don't want. That image often puts prospective customers off even making an enquiry. Start to take notice now of how many advertisements for major products, while inviting the prospective customer to write or phone for a brochure, add: 'No salesperson will call.'

Today, the professional and intelligent approach to sales is to

LISTEN.

Listen to what the customer has to say. Give them a chance to say it. You have to listen to what the prospective customer is saying in order to discover what benefits they are seeking. If you can get the customer to talk, you can find out what their needs and desires are.

You might be able to encourage the customer to talk by prompting them with the right questions. The more you can get them to chat, the more likely they will reveal their psychological desires, such as enhanced status. By listening to what prospective customers say and discovering their needs and desires, you can then match these to the benefits that your product offers and make it clear to the customer that your product offers what they want.

This was the approach taken by *Lee* when he set up his intruder alarm business specialising in alarms for the home. Here's what he had to say about how this approach worked for him:

I soon learnt to listen carefully to what my potential customers were saying. An intruder alarm system has a lot of benefits to offer but they're not all sought by every customer. So for example, one customer mentioned to me early on in my visit that his sister had bought an intruder alarm and it had turned out to be unreliable. That guy was clearly looking for a system which would offer reliability and so during my presentation I made sure I emphasised the features of the system that reduced the incidences of false alarms. I got the order, although the guy had received two quotes from another firm, one of which was cheaper than mine.

Another potential customer whom I visited to give a quote opened the door and told me I was lucky to catch them in at the weekend because they went away in their caravan most weekends. What that told me was they had premises that were often left unattended for two or three days at a time. So later on I pointed out to them that some premises had a greater need than others for an alarm system and this included premises that were left unoccupied on a regular basis. I could tell from the guy's expression that he had taken what I'd said on board and was thinking that the point applied to them: they had a greater need than other people for an alarm.

Of course some people are less chatty than others and so you might need to ask questions to elicit information that's useful. But you might have to frame those questions in such a way that it's not too obvious to the customer what you are trying to do. I'm trying to make a sale of an item that sells for between £300 and £500, so it's worth my spending time with the customer. I find it helps to get them chatting (and thus revealing what it is they want) and feeling relaxed. So if they offer me a cup of tea or coffee I always say yes, as they are more likely to chat over tea of coffee.

Not only should you listen to prospective customers but you should make sure you give the impression that you are doing so. This is particularly important when the customer is raising objections, giving you reasons why they might not buy. To help show that I've been listening carefully to the point they are making, I pause slightly before replying. I don't want to give the prospective customer the impression that I'm just glibly replying with our standard response. However, I do want to be prepared to deal with objections, so when I first started selling my alarms I sat down and tried to think up possible objections a customer might have to buying from me. Every so often, of course, a customer will come up with a new reason why the system isn't suitable for them or why they shouldn't buy at that point in time. I make sure I add it to my list and I go over in my head what my response was on that occasion in case I could improve on it for next time.

As business has been quite good, I recently decided to treat myself to a new stereo system. The guy in the store hardly paused for breath. I was surprised that there were still salespeople like that. He talked so much, it was getting on my nerves. I had a really strong urge to tell him to talk less, and to listen and think more. I ended up buying it somewhere else even though their prices were a bit higher.

ADVERTS

Before you get to the point of being able to make a sale, your potential customer has to be aware that your business exists. In Chapter 13 we looked at ways in which you could do this either at low cost or no cost.

But maybe you have some budget to spend on advertising. It's unlikely your budget will extend to TV advertising, so your thoughts will probably turn to newspapers and magazines. Depending on the nature of your product or service, it may be that you confine yourself to local advertising. If you prune and cut down trees for householders, even if your budget would extend to it, it's probably a waste of money to advertise in a national magazine and receive responses from Mr and Mrs Jones who live 200 miles away. Naturally, it would be different if you had a product that you could send to them.

In the first year of operating his intruder alarm system business, Lee learnt some valuable lessons about paid-for advertising.

Getting the advert right is a real trial-and-error thing. Certainly in the market I'm in, selling to consumers, I've learnt that getting the wording right is a real hit and miss game. I used to think that professionals – advertising agencies and copywriters – would always get it right but I don't think they do. You can't be sure how people will react to an advert. I was really lucky and a small ad I put in the local paper worked in the first month.

I've learnt that most people buying intruder alarms are likely to be fairly prudent. A lot of my customers are middle class and many are in the older age group. I realise now that some of the wording I used in that first ad particularly appealed to them.

We used the expression 'very reasonable' about the likely costs and I think that worked well. These weren't people who were necessarily looking for a bargain or the cheapest but they did want value for money. So the ad worked.

But then I made a mistake. I wanted to see if I could get an even better response even though the one I was getting was good. So at the end of three months when it came to renew the advertisement I changed the wording. It was incredible: the response just dried up. Although it was only a small change in the text of the advertisement, about what we could offer. After the ad had appeared three times without any callers I panicked and told the girl that I usually dealt with in the advertising department to change the wording back. I still don't know why the change put people off and had learnt the lesson that advertising can be a hit and miss affair.

After we'd been operating for about a year I was tempted to try another change in the wording. Same result! Again after a couple of inserts I asked them to change the wording back. There is some truth in the saying that "if it isn't broke, don't fix it!"

I also learnt this valuable lesson. The sort of market I was in consisted of local householders, respectable, ordinary hard-working people. They liked the fact they were buying from a local business. They also liked the fact that I advertised every week in the local paper. It was a very small ad and it didn't cost much at all. Talking to customers made me realise that being in the local paper every week gave these people a degree of security and confidence in dealing with my firm. So you may find that some of your potential customers don't respond until they have seen your advertisement many times and that the number of enquiries from the ad builds up over time. Even if the response is a bit disappointing in the early weeks it doesn't mean to say that the advertisement is a complete flop. You may have to stay with it for a while.

I've also learnt that some of the cheapest advertising can be the most effective. Many localities, especially villages, have a parish newsletter, usually published by a local church or a community centre. Advertising in one of these can be incredibly cheap. A whole year's advertising in a parish newsletter covering three villages cost me £36 a year and during that year I must have made seven or eight sales from it. Again, the first few times it appeared I only got one or two enquiries. But now I'm in half a dozen parish magazines every month and they bring in a steady trickle of enquiries.

When it comes to drafting the wording for the advertisement, don't forget that customers buy benefits – they want to know what the product or service will do for them. So a useful approach to get you started is to make a list of the benefits your product or service offers. Which of those benefits would be the most important to the typical reader of that particular newspaper or magazine? Put those high on your list and put at the top of the list any such benefit you offer that helps you stand out from the competition, perhaps because your competitors don't offer it or it's something new.

That word 'new' is one of the most powerful words in advertising. But probably the word with the greatest pulling power is 'free.' Lee's advertisements for his intruder alarm systems offer prospective customers a FREE no-obligation quote and a FREE security check of their premises – but he makes sure he costs it into the price!

CLOSE THAT DEAL

Closing the sale – going for the order – requires a bit of courage, because none of us likes rejection. But there are proven, effective techniques you can use to get the customer to say 'yes' and these can boost your confidence.

The right approach is to *lead* your prospective customer into doing the deal. Here are some of the techniques.

Turning round an objection: When your customer comes up with an objection, a reason why they can't buy, this could be a good opportunity for you to close the sale. If you can deal with their objection, demolish it, and demonstrate to your customer that their fears are answered, then this should impress them. And that's a good moment to nod encouragingly and give them an expectant look!

The summary: If the customer hasn't raised an objection, try this approach. Summarise briefly the benefits you have set out for the customer – all the benefits that have emerged and which will apply to them if they purchase your product or service. This demonstrates there is simply nothing left to be dealt with. With all those benefits, surely they are going to place an order?

The fear close: This is probably the most popular, widely used technique for getting the order. You make it clear to the customer that a benefit will be *lost* if the customer does not go ahead. An example of this is the special offer with a time limit: if they don't place their order within seven days – today is the last day – they won't get free weekend texts, or whatever. Or: this is the last one in stock and we don't know when the next delivery will be – and there might even be a price increase when the next lot comes in! The 'fear close' gives you lots of options, so think about what could apply to your product or service. This can be the most effective close of all, as we don't like to lose things that we could have had.

The alternatives: This approach is more subtle. You put a question to the prospective customer that makes them choose between two alternatives. You formulate the question so that by answering and opting for one of the alternatives the customer is committing themselves. Example: 'We could do delivery after Christmas if it would you suit you to wait – or would you prefer delivery in time for Christmas?'

Getting the sale can leave you with a very satisfied feeling of achievement. Especially if it's your own business!

CHAPTER 16
WHICH BUSINESS IDEA?

As you've been working through this second part of the book, it's very likely that your list of possibilities for a new business to start has been whittled down. It could be that your market research has caused you to cross off one of the ideas from the list, perhaps after you've looked at the competition or failed to work out a price that would give you the profit you need.

In the next chapter, we'll be suggesting you make a start on writing your business plan. You won't want to waste time writing more than one, so you'll need to have settled on your business idea by then. Although many of the issues we've looked at so far will have helped you to evaluate the ideas you've been considering, here we'll set out some other factors you need to take into account when deciding which idea to go with. You can, of course, seek professional advice from Business Link, your local enterprise agency and perhaps the Prince's Trust. You may also need – or want – to seek the input of an accountant or your bank.

GETTING SUPPLIES

It's possible that your business will be making the product you sell. Craft items, foodstuffs and clothing all lend themselves to small-scale manufacturing. We assume you'll be starting small-scale because it's unlikely that you have – or can raise – sufficient capital to build oil tankers or mass produce cars. Just because your first batch of products is produced in the tiniest unit at the local council's starter units for new small businesses doesn't mean it couldn't grow to be the new Adidas, Innocent or Rimmel.

But, most probably, you'll be buying in your product. Even if your business is a service business, it's likely that customers will be receiving from you more than just your labour. For example a mobile mechanic offering car repairs and servicing will also supply replacement components. So most businesses will be relying to some extent on others for their product. Where will you find these good products?

TRACKING DOWN SUPPLIERS

Sometimes items that you expect to be easy to source turn out not to be so. For her first product, *Samantha* needed to source a tiny bear from a supplier of soft toys, jars of organic honey and a gold cardboard box in which to present the honey and the bear. Of the three, the most difficult to find a supplier for was the cardboard box in the specification she needed. We've already noted earlier some possibilities for locating suppliers: trade journals, trade exhibitions and overseas trade promotion bodies. Your local Business Link can probably provide a list of possible suppliers and your local reference library may hold a directory of suppliers, listing suppliers by trade. On the Internet you'll find a number of commercial organisations that can supply information about what's available from manufacturers, wholesalers and importers and keep you abreast of new product launches or offers, a service for which you can expect to pay a subscription.

Lack of continuity of supply can be a source of exasperation. Success in business involves much more than simply locating a product that sells profitably. Perhaps you were really pleased to find that line in oversize watches which sold really well. So you place another order with your supplier for three times as many as you bought initially, only to find they haven't got any – oversize watches have suddenly become very popular and they've sold out. And you get really wound up when another supplier withdraws a line from their catalogue and doesn't tell you – and you've just taken an order for it from a customer. So even if you have found what you think is the best source of supply, do consider keeping a second supplier in tow. You could place the occasional order with Alternative Supplier Ltd so as to have another possible source of supply when your usual suppliers let you down.

PREMISES, PREMISES
Will your business need a roof over its head?

Perhaps you have a spare room at home that's just waiting for you to use it. Or, if not, maybe you don't even need a whole room to begin with. We've known businesses that were launched in a corner of the bedroom. But if you can't even spare that – because you share it with your brother/sister – and you can't afford the rent for premises, there are other possibilities.

Emma, who started a business wholesaling novelty gifts, set up in…a caravan! Emma still lived at home, in a house with a long garden. She bought an old but structurally sound caravan for £350 from an ad in the local paper. Sited at the bottom of the garden, it gave her somewhere to use as an office for a few hours a week. Within four months, the turnover and profit from her business was enough to enable her to pay a small rent for a small unit on a local industrial estate and her dad subsequently used the caravan for storing his garden tools and sacks of peat.

Or could you get started by using the garage? Yes we know, your mum and dad use it for parking the car, or perhaps it's full of clutter. How about offering to clear it out, selling what is no longer wanted – which is probably nearly all of it – at a car-boot sale, then splitting the proceeds 50–50 with your parents. That way you'll also have a bit of money to put towards starting your business.

And we've known two or three small business that started life in a garden shed – you can buy one for just £200–£300.

We're assuming you'll only use these makeshift premises on a part-time basis, perhaps as somewhere to store goods, and only as a temporary solution. We're not suggesting you open a shop or run a car repairs and servicing business from the caravan at the bottom of your garden. Not least because you don't want to fall out with the neighbours. Even if you've not been concerned about upsetting Mr and Mrs Negative next door before, you'll now have to be concerned about the reputation of your business. You don't want them bad-mouthing you to other people who might be potential customers. And the people in your street might be potential customers, so you don't want to upset them by operating noisy machinery at 8 o'clock on a Sunday morning.

And then, of course, there are legal considerations, most notably the planning laws. Do you need planning permission from the local council? At present, the house or flat you live in will have planning permission for use as a dwelling, but probably not for use as a business. If you want to use your home – or part of your home – as business premises, you may have to obtain planning permission for change of use. It's not easy to answer here with a definite yes or no as whether you will need permission depends upon your particular circumstances and the nature and scale of the work you do.

Thousands of people probably use their home to some small extent for the purposes of business and do not need planning permission to do so. Permission would be required, though, for a 'material' change of use. If the premises were no longer used primarily for living in, then you'd definitely have to seek permission. At the other end of the scale, someone who works as a freelance insurance agent probably won't need planning permission to use a study at home for a few hours each week to do their books. To what extent will your home be used for business purposes? Will such use be substantial?

The planning officer from the local council will consider whether there has been a marked rise in callers at the house. They will have to take into account the amount of extra traffic resulting from your business activities. Is there a succession of car doors slamming? Lorries with noisy diesel engines? If your customers' cars or suppliers' delivery vans block your neighbour's driveway, your neighbour is likely to pick up the phone and complain to the local council.

If you have doubts about whether or not you need planning permission, contact the planning department at your local authority and ask for guidance. Some planning departments are often quite supportive of small businesses who are struggling to take root from the proprietor's home address. But this sympathetic, generous interpretation of the planning laws could give way to a stricter interpretation once your new business has a foothold and with it the income to pay rent for the business premises you need.

There are also other legal considerations. It's possible there is what is called a 'restrictive covenant' in the deeds of the property that prohibits use of the property for business purposes and this could be used against you by an antagonistic neighbour. Particularly with modern housing estates it's not uncommon to find that the deeds of the property include a clause prohibiting use of the property for business purposes. And if you live in rented accommodation, check whether you need the landlord's permission to run a business from there. There may be a clause in your tenancy agreement which either prohibits business use or makes it subject to the landlord's permission, so read your copy of the agreement carefully.

COMMERCIAL PREMISES

If your business idea is one that leaves you no choice other than to operate from commercial premises, you'll discover that the problem for many new businesses is finding premises that are affordable. Again, we have some suggestions that have worked for others before you.

Start in the usual way by looking at the advertisements in the commercial property column of your local paper. However, not all empty property is advertised for rent. So ask around to see if any friends or relatives know of someone who has spare space but has perhaps never bothered to rent it out. You might unearth modest business premises at a very reasonable rent. The economic recession that began in 2008 caused many firms to cut back on their activities, often shedding staff in the process. Your local high street probably accommodates a number of small businesses working out of offices located above shops – is it possible that one of these firms now has an empty room or two on the top floor? Do you or your friends or your parents or other relatives have contacts you could talk to? You might discover that your friend's father runs a small business and has a room that's not used.

Take the initiative and pay for a small 'accommodation wanted' ad in the local paper. And don't dismiss advertising in that most inexpensive of media: your newsagent's noticeboard. Your ad should stand out among the other cards offering second-hand pushchairs for sale and rewards for lost cats. Make the ad an appeal for help. Word it along the lines of 'new small business needs somewhere to work from at a rent a young entrepreneur could afford'.

We know of a firm of solicitors who responded to such an ad. The basement of their premises was considered insufficiently grand to be used as offices for meeting clients and so was standing empty. The three rooms in the basement were starting to get musty. The young tenant could have the use of them at a very low rent if he was prepared to give the rooms a coat of paint – and keep the garden tidy.

In order to encourage business start-ups, many local councils and enterprise agencies offer 'nursery' units. These are small premises offered for rent to businesses who are starting up or in their early years. The units are commonly let on an 'easy in, easy out' basis. There's no long-term commitment as you'd expect with a lease on ordinary commercial premises: if things don't work out you can usually give just one or two months' notice to quit the premises. Your local council will have a department that encourages business development in the area, so get in touch with them to see if they operate such a scheme.

If you have the funds to afford traditional commercial premises, you should seek professional legal advice before entering into an agreement, so get yourself a solicitor. But if, as with most young people starting a business, money is tight and you need bargain-priced premises, then you'll have to find an alternative solution. If you're determined enough, you'll find a way.

PERMISSION?

We've mentioned that planning permission is one legal matter you'll have to consider; another is whether or not you have to obtain permission to operate your business.

Check out if you need a licence for your new business. As a general rule, in our free enterprise society you won't need to apply for a licence to set up in business. The basic principle is that any person is free to set up and operate a lawful business without requiring the consent of HM government.

However, as you might expect, this general freedom is subject to a number of exceptions. Some of these, you're probably already familiar with. For example, if you wish to operate as a bookmaker, or to retail alcohol, you'll have to get a licence. You might also need a licence to run your business in a particular manner; for example, if you will be making door-to-door sales.

And although your business might not require a licence to operate, one or more of your business *activities* could be subject to some form of licensing. For instance, you don't need a licence to set up retailing lawn mowers, but if you wanted to sell these to consumers on credit, then you must be licensed under the consumer credit laws. And your local council might have its own licensing requirements for a particular trade operating in its locality. A local authority has power to make by-laws for its area and some councils use these to regulate business activities.

If all this sounds a lot to find out about, don't worry. These are exactly the sort of issues that Business Link and/or your local enterprise agency can help with. Tell them the business you have in mind and how you plan to operate it.

They'll also be able to give you advice on whether you need a particular qualification to operate your business or if you need to belong to some regulatory body. Most trades have a professional association, open to members of that trade and, in practice, even if there is no legal requirement to join the association, it may be to your advantage to do so. For instance, the association might offer an insurance scheme especially for their members that would save you money. Saving you money has to be a good idea!

TWO RELATED CONSIDERATIONS

When deciding whether your business idea is a viable one, you need to give some thought to the following issues: complexity and complaints.

The more complex your product or service, the more factors you'll have to take on board. So, if your new business were to be product-based, you'd have to take into account how difficult it would be to make, install or fit it. And the greater its complexity, the more technical skills – or assistance – you'll need to carry out these functions. This was something *Lee* had to deal with when he set up his intruder alarm systems business. Lee had good sales and marketing skills and his order book was filling up, but he wasn't good at technical work. And fitting the alarms – drilling, screwing, and wiring-up – didn't appeal to him, so right from the start he realised he'd need someone to help him with that side of the business.

When running your own small business, you'll have to turn your hand to this and that: some of the tasks you will enjoy, one or two of them may bore you, and there are likely to be others that you dread. So, rather than take on the tasks you dread, and perhaps do them badly, it would be better to spend your time on some other aspect of the business and enlist the aid of another pair of hands. But what happens if the figures indicate that the business wouldn't be able to afford to pay somebody else to do what the boss can't? Also, what are the chances of your finding someone in your area who could do this work?

The more complex the product or service, the more chances there are for mistakes to be made. There's a big difference between running a business that sells a standardised, simple product and one which sells, installs and maintains an electronic burglar alarm system in a five-bedroomed house. If you like a quiet life and don't want lots of responsibility and/or are not good at resolving problems when things go wrong, maybe you should avoid a business with a complex product or service, especially one where you couldn't deal with the technical side of things.

Lee's alarm systems were installed for him by a self-employed electrician working as a sub-contractor. If the system malfunctioned, it was the sub-contractor's number that customers telephoned. But even then Lee has to admit: 'It was amazing how often alarms would go wrong when the electrician was on holiday!' Contrast that with a business which supplies a simple, uniform product. In a small business you cannot pass the complaining customer from department to department; the buck stops at the proprietor's desk – your desk. But if your product is a standard item that you keep in stock, when the complaining customer drops it on your desk you can simply take a replacement from the shelf to appease them.

Remember how, early in the book, we said you needed to come up with a business idea that suited you, and that suited your personality? This is an example of why you need to do that.

DOES SIZE MATTER TO YOU?

Some of the matters we've raised in this chapter may have caused you to furrow your brow. Lots of things to think about? Is that going to be a big problem? Is setting up going to be too much of a headache? Are you now thinking that perhaps you won't set up in business after all? Are you tempted to turn to the sits-vac column of the local paper?

But if you get a job, you will still have complications at work that you'll have to deal with. And things you have to do during the day that you don't like doing. Perhaps it's time to turn back to the early chapters of the book and remind yourself of some of the benefits you could get from having your own business and being your own boss.

And, in evaluating your business idea, here's something more pleasurable to take account of and dwell upon. It involves thinking about your future. This question will again take you back to the early part of the book and the central issue of what type of business you want. Ask yourself: how far do I want my business to grow? How ambitious are you? A business where you are – and always will be – the only person working in it? A small business with a handful of people working with you? A multinational operation that changes the world?

If you have a huge ambition, but your product or service has only a very limited market, perhaps you will need to move on to the next idea. Or will you? Maybe you could set up this business, with its limited market, and later use some of the profits from that to start a second enterprise that has a big potential. Perhaps you would like to run two – or three or four or more – enterprises. Goodness knows how many Richard Branson runs!

However, whether your business grows – and how fast – is not entirely within your control. If one of those external factors we looked at earlier – such as public opinion or government policy – changes, you might find your business suddenly grows on the back of this change (or shrinks). The constant process of change keeps all businesses guessing. When you start up a business, it is impossible to predict exactly where it may lead you.

But then that is part of the excitement.

CHAPTER 17
YOUR PLAN FOR YOUR BUSINESS

If you've worked your way through all the issues we've looked at so far, your future plans should be taking shape and you'll have already done much of the preparatory work needed to write your business plan. This is a document which sets down in writing what type of business yours will be, what you hope to achieve, how you'll set up and run the business, and other relevant information. If putting pen to paper is not your favourite task, take comfort from this: if your business idea is fairly straightforward, your plan need only be a few pages long. Should you require a more detailed plan, you can ask your bank or business counsellor for a business plan pack which contains pre-printed forms and templates. Just fill in the relevant sections and you'll have a completed business plan. However, we believe there are good reasons for you to make the effort to write your own plan – unless the thought of doing so gives you a real headache. If writing doesn't come easy to you, maybe you could enlist someone's help? While you might want – or need – to keep what you're doing confidential, is there a close relative or a really good friend who could help?

This is going to be YOUR business. A business that you have devised that will suit YOU. This is about YOUR future. This is YOUR plan. So instead of using a standard form drawn up by someone else, why not put in the effort to produce a document of which YOU are proud.

WHAT GOES IN IT?

The details that are usually covered in a business plan include the following.

- What sort of business it will be.

- Who you are, plus information about any business partners who will be working with you.

- Who you will be selling to and what the competition is.

- The turnover and profits you expect the business to achieve.

- How much money you'll need to start the business and what it will be used for.

- How much money you'll need to cover day-to-day costs (cash flow).

- What you'll be doing to get the business launched and how you will run the business.

If you wish, you can add an appendix or appendices to your business plan. For instance, you could include a copy of a leaflet you have designed.

If this sounds a lot to think and write about, here's another advantage to think about. Writing a business plan that sets out the above facts, however briefly, will act as a checklist to help ensure you've thought of all the things you need to think about and haven't left out any key information. If you have missed something, it's better to realise now and get it sorted than find out five days – or months – into your new business!

It's also likely that you'll be showing your business plan to professional bodies. For example, if you apply for a bank loan, your bank will certainly expect to see a formal business plan as proof that you've thought matters through. And if you're planning to set up a fairly large-scale operation and need the capital to match, you might want to approach other professional providers of finance for business start-ups; these investors provide what is commonly called venture capital. Venture capitalists often invest in higher risk businesses but, accordingly, expect a higher return. They will usually want to part-own the business and, often, to have a role in management. In practice, the overwhelming majority of businesses started by young people don't need to be involved with venture capitalists but if yours does then they will want to see a detailed document that gives them the confidence to get financially involved.

YOU

The order in which you set down the information in your business plan is up to you, although you should start by describing who you are and what your business will entail. Note down any paper qualifications you have – professional or academic – as well as any relevant experience and useful skills. To jog your memory, check the answers you provided in your *Who am I?* questionnaire. And don't be shy – don't exaggerate, but do include details of what you've done and what you know that could be useful in running the business.

As other people will be reading your plan, such as the business counsellor at your local enterprise agency or Business Link or the business adviser at your bank, break it down under headings to make it easier to read. So, the heading for the first section could simply be 'Introduction' or 'Overview'.

LEGAL STRUCTURE

Will you operate as a sole trader, a partnership or a registered company? These are the principal choices open to you, so weigh up these options in the light of your personal circumstances and what you're good at and not so good at. Also, take into account the size of your business and the specific tasks that will need to be carried out.

If you're planning a small-scale operation, you might decide to operate as a sole trader. The business would be all your responsibility but, on the plus side, you'd be the boss.

Or will you need a business partner? Actually, it's not just a question of need, would you *like* to work with a partner – have someone with whom you can share the decision-making and talk things over? But then, what if there were only two of you and you couldn't agree on some important matter? There are both advantages and disadvantages in having a business partner.

When you have your own business you won't have a boss looking over your shoulder, making sure you get in on time and start your work promptly. So how good are you at getting up in the morning? If you had a business partner who was an early riser, they might be ringing you at 8:30 a.m. to discuss the day's work – and then arrive at work at 8.55 a.m. to get started. That could be especially beneficial if *you* are not normally an early riser.

But if that sounds useful, here's something that may cause you to pause for thought: you might be liable for any debts that your business partner incurred on behalf of the business. You could also be liable in law for any other actions your business partner took on behalf of the business. You would have to trust this person.

Even if you've been best mates since you were 11 years old, there's one thing in particular you could fall out over – money. There are so many potential legal implications or complications that a business partnership isn't something you can simply agree on by shaking hands with your mate over a drink in the pub. Seek professional help and have a properly drawn-up partnership agreement, setting out the rights and responsibilities of each partner. A solicitor will do this for you and, yes, you will have to pay for it, but in the long run it could save you a lot of money – as well as arguments, worry and regrets.

Unless you get things sorted beforehand, here are a few examples of what you might be saying to each other in a few months' time:

'Why should you get 50 per cent of the profits? I bring in 75 per cent of the money!'

'Why should I have to split the profits with you when I put in more hours and do more work than you?'

'This isn't right, you taking half the profits. Most of the profits come from people who have only become clients because I know them. You've hardly brought in any clients.'

'This isn't fair. Why am I working evenings and Saturdays and you're not?'

'It's only right that you should do more work than me, because I put in more capital than you. We wouldn't have been able to start this business if I hadn't provided most of the money we needed.'

'You had no right to sign that contract to lease a BMW for the business. We could have managed with a cheaper car. You just want to ride around in a flash car – while I help pay for it.'

'You shouldn't have drawn that much out of the bank.'

The third possibility is the registered company. Legally speaking, this is very different from a partnership. But, as with a partnership, opting to trade as a registered company is not something you should enter into lightly. At first sight it seems very attractive. A company has a membership and the members can have limited liability – so their liability for any debts incurred by the company is limited. Our free enterprise system wishes to encourage people to invest in business, and a limited company is a way in which they can do so without the risk of exposing themselves to untold losses – their liability is limited to the investment they put in. (It's also possible for a partner in a partnership to have limited liability, but a limited company is the usual way of providing for this.)

You can register a new limited company or you can buy a ready-made one off the shelf. In either case many people use the services of a 'company registration agent', as using such a specialist is normally a quicker route to having your own company. Before making your decision, there are many important issues to consider. Perhaps you need to bring a number of people into your business to make it work, or because it's a new product or a new market there's a lot of financial risk involved, and so a limited liability company could be right for your business. Do get advice from a professional, who can take into account your particular circumstances. Talk it over with a business counsellor, accountant, solicitor or bank adviser – or all of them.

ANOTHER PAIR OF HANDS

If we could read your mind as you read this book, we would know the scale of the business operation you are planning. If your plan is for the smallest of operations, you may not need to have anyone working in the business with you. But if other people are to be involved, you must include them – who they are and the role they will play – in your business plan.

If you require help in running your business, you might think the most obvious step, apart from having a business partner, is to take on an employee. But taking on an employee, even if only on a part-time basis, means taking on extra responsibilities. You may have to operate a Pay As You Earn (PAYE) scheme, which involves deducting income tax and National Insurance contributions from your employee's pay, as well as paying Employer's National Insurance Contributions. Employees have certain rights – such as the right to sickness pay, holiday pay, maternity/paternity leave, and so on – and, although as a small business you might be exempt from some obligations, you'll have to find out about them and which ones you would have to comply with. And then there's all the health and safety legislation. If you choose to go down the route of becoming an employer, familiarise yourself with your legal duties and make sure you comply with them.

But there are alternatives to taking on an employee. Could you get some members of your family to help out? Even if it's only for the first few months, just to get you going. Don't expect everyone to step in, though: your parents might be pleased to help out, but your big, strapping brother might be reluctant! If your mum were to put pressure on him and his attitude was 'I'm doing you a favour', this would be reflected in the way he dealt with customers, for instance in his tone of voice when answering the phone. Better to work with enthusiastic volunteers rather than grumpy conscripts.

Another alternative to taking on an employee – and all the legal obligations that go with it – or using a reluctant relative, is to pay someone to do the work, someone who doesn't become an employee. A person who performs work for another in return for payment, but who is not an employee, is in the eyes of the law an *independent contractor*. If you think about it, we all use other people to perform work for us in return for payment and yet they are not our employees, such as the self-employed window cleaner who calls once a month or the gardener who cuts the lawn once a week.

Once you set up your business, you will be using independent contractors anyway – such as the decorator who paints your office and the courier who delivers your parcels. So maybe your business could use independent contractors to carry out some of your other work and save you taking on an employee.

That was the solution that Lee chose in his intruder alarm business. Lee couldn't be sure how many alarms would need to be fitted in any particular month so, rather than paying a full-time fitter and risk not having enough work for them, he used the services of a self-employed electrician. The only drawback was that, as the electrician had other clients, he was sometimes too busy to undertake a fitting for Lee when it was needed. The solution was to use more than one contractor and split the work between them.

PROTECTING THE BUSINESS

Say the word 'insurance' to most people and their eyes glaze over. Many people – especially young people – don't just find it boring, but complicated, too. And expensive. So we say: demonstrate your maturity and your professionalism by showing in your business plan that you are aware of the risks to which the business is exposed and have taken steps to cover them. It's not true that if you don't make a claim you will have wasted your money. What you buy and receive is peace of mind.

You might need insurance for:

■ product liability – what if you sell a customer shampoo and it makes their hair fall out?

■ stock – what if somebody nicks it?

■ occupier's liability – what if a sales rep visiting your premises trips on a loose stair carpet and breaks his leg?

■ goods in transit – what if they're smashed?

■ premises

■ equipment

■ injuries to employees

■ breaching employee rights

■ injuries to customers – what if, as part of your garden maintenance service, you cut a branch off a tree and it drops on to the customers head?

The good news is that many insurers offer small-business insurance packages: a single policy offers cover for a menu of risks from which you make a selection appropriate to your needs. You might even get a pleasant surprise. One young guy who set up a garden maintenance service trawled the Internet and found an insurance broker who offered a comprehensive package for just £95 a year. And that included claims by customers for up to a quarter of a million pounds! We've also had good reports about the insurance service offered by the Federation of Small Businesses (FSB), whose deals are tailored for the self-employed and small enterprises. In any case, check out their website (**www.fsb.org.uk**) for details of the range of benefits that membership offers to small businesses, including help with legal and tax problems – which can be very reassuring to have.

HOW MUCH?

When you start a business, there are two money questions that will loom large. How much? And how do I get it?

You will need finance for:

- start-up costs, such as the costs of paying a solicitor to draft a partnership agreement;

- acquiring assets which the business expects to use and retain for some time (these are called fixed assets), such as office furniture – the capital required for fixed assets is known as fixed capital;

- the regular outgoings of the business, such as payments for petrol, telephone, stock – this is known as working capital.

How much working capital you will need depends on how many sales you make and how long it takes to convert the cash you've laid out on stock and other outgoings back into cash when the customer pays you.

Please take the following valuable lesson on board: *a business can make profits and yet still go under*. How can this be? It can happen because your customers are slow in paying you and, while you're waiting, you have to find the money to pay the people and businesses *you* owe money to (creditors). Your biggest and most profitable customer might keep you waiting for four months before they pay your account, but you can't keep the phone company waiting for four months before you pay their account – they will cut the phone off. And what if your supplier of stock refuses to process your current order because they haven't been paid yet for goods previously supplied?

Your cash flow is all important. Cash flow refers to the money coming into and going out of the business. Money due to you must be rolling in for you to be able to pay it out again on your bills.

If you're hoping your business plan will convince some individual or organisation to make you a loan, or possibly a grant, you will have to provide them with a forecast of the cash flow you expect your business to have. This cash-flow forecast is usually set out as an appendix to your business plan. Even if you're not using one of those pre-prepared business plan documents where you fill in the information in the space provided, you might find it useful to use the cash-flow forecast from that. This will set out the money you expect to come into the business and the monthly payments you expect to make. Of course you don't know yet how much money will be coming in, because you don't know how many sales you will be making, so you will have to estimate this.

For many people setting up a business for the first time, the prospect of estimating their cash flow seems a hopeless task: how can you give a realistic figure for the amount of money that will come in during the first few months of the business? Well, your market research might at least give you some idea for now and there's a good reason for trying. Once you start trading, as you get the real figures in, you can compare them with the figures you forecast. As the months go by, your forecast can be adjusted for the future in the light of the actual performance.

You will know what some of the figures are for outgoings because they'll be the same every month. These will include items such as insurance or rent, for example. Other payments may vary, depending on the volume of business you are doing, such as diesel for the van. The latter will be difficult to predict with great accuracy, but you can make a reasonable estimate and, as we have seen, modify it later in the light of experience.

The cash-flow forecast is also a way of working out what is called your 'break-even' figure. This is the turnover in sales you must achieve in order to be able to meet your financial commitments. After break-even, you start to make a profit. But how long will this take? And do you have enough finance to get you there?

One thing you may not need to bother about just yet, until your turnover reaches a certain annual figure, is VAT (Value Added Tax). The level of turnover at which you have to start charging VAT to customers is determined by the government and it changes from time to time (usually once a year). To find out the current level of turnover at which you must charge VAT, check the website for HM Revenue & Customs (formerly the Inland Revenue): **www.hmrc.gov.uk**. The VAT you collect from customers is then passed on to HMRC after you've deducted the VAT that you've paid out yourself on purchases for the business.

So yes, the dreaded 'tax' word has crept in. When you operate a business, tax is payable on the profits of that business. Your profit is what you have left after deducting your expenditure, but a complication arises where some expenditure has been incurred partly for yourself and partly for the business. An example would be a repair bill on your car, where you use your car both for private use and for the business. Thus some of your expenditure will be apportioned as being partly for business purposes and partly for your personal benefit.

As soon as you begin incurring expenditure for the business – including pre-launch expenditure in planning the business, such as buying this book – think: RECEIPT!

Your accountant will tell you what items are allowable for tax purposes, but if in doubt always get a receipt – and hang on to it. Broadly speaking, the usual expenses of running a business can be offset, such as:

■ printing

■ stationery

■ telephone

■ transport

■ postage

- insurance

- bank charges

- trade journals

- repairs to equipment

- advertising

When you set up in business, you must notify HM Revenue & Customs within three months.

RAISING THE MONEY

Having worked out how much money you will need, the big question is where will you get it from?

Depending on your circumstances, you might be able to obtain some limited financial help from the Prince's Trust (**www.princes-trust.org.uk**). The Prince's Trust Business Programme offers advice and training for business start-ups for 18 to 30-year-olds who are working fewer than 16 hours a week. The Shell LiveWIRE programme (**www.shell-livewire.org**) runs a 'Grand Ideas Award', which offers young entrepreneurs the chance to win up to £1,000 to help get their business off the ground. Otherwise, you could approach your bank for a loan. If that doesn't seem feasible or the bank's representative says 'No' or they've recently asked you to cut up your debit card and return it to them, here are some alternatives.

■ *Another idea:* As we suggested earlier, if you come up with a business idea that requires more capital than you can raise, don't bin the idea. Put it to one side for now and try to come up with another idea that requires less capital. If this is successful, you can then use some of the profits from that business to go back to your Big Idea.

■ *Look again at your costs:* You might be used to buying new stuff for yourself, but couldn't the photocopier or computer you need for your business be a reconditioned one – at a fraction of the price? And if you require special equipment or fittings for your particular trade, there are specialist suppliers that offer reconditioned machinery, such as that industrial sewing machine you need. If you are considering, say, a catering business, the cost of commercial kitchen equipment might raise your eyebrows – but so too might the low price obtained for it at an auction 18 months later when some new restaurant folded. Find out about auctions from your local and regional newspapers and the Internet. Buying second-hand equipment will raise your green credentials and you will make good use of its remaining lifespan.

■ *Savings:* If you have savings, you might be reluctant to raid them, but it wouldn't have to be a non-repayable raid. Make a loan to yourself on the basis that you'll pay it back over a period of time out of the profits of the business. Of course, there's a chance your profits might not be sufficient to enable you to make the repayments, in which case it would be better to just dip in to your savings rather than emptying the pot completely.

■ *Liquidate an asset:* We're using the language of financiers here. In fact, all we're doing is pointing out that most of us have some item that we could – or ought to – sell but have never got round to it. It could be a gadget that proved to be a disappointment. Or that extravagant impulse purchase you made and hardly ever used, or something bought for a hobby for which your enthusiasm has faded? Perhaps members of your family have got stuff they could sell, too? If you haven't got enough of your own items to make a trip to the car-boot fair worthwhile, offer to take their unwanted goods and split the proceeds. Some of the items might be worth putting on eBay.

■ *Get other people you know to 'invest':* Perhaps Mum or Dad or Auntie Mary/Uncle Jack or your grandparents would consider giving you a loan? Is it possible they've been putting some money aside for you which was going to come to you at a later date? Could they dip into that now to help fund this investment in your future? As mentioned earlier, it is possible for your new enterprise to take the legal form of a registered company. If you are planning a larger-scale enterprise that requires a sizeable amount of capital, you could form or buy a ready-made company in which relatives and/or friends buy shares without exposing themselves to liability for the debts of the business. Would your grandparents be prepared to sell their shares in BT and reinvest in shares in your business, merely exchanging one investment for another? One advantage of using a limited company is that the lump sum you need, which might be more than a single investor would be happy to risk, could be put together from sales of shares to a number of friends and acquaintances happy to gamble, say, a couple of hundred pounds.

■ *Customers:* Yes, your customers could help finance your new business. Is your product or service one where you could seek prepayment from customers? You should certainly consider requesting a deposit if your business is one that requires you to make an outlay on materials in order to carry out work for the customer. We know a business that makes cakes for weddings and other special occasions and requests a deposit of 50 per cent with the order. The young proprietor reports that, in four years of trading, only a handful of customers have quibbled at this.

■ *Supplier credit:* If your business provides products rather than services, your biggest recurring expenditure will probably be on stock, in which case you may find it difficult to pay – either on ordering or on delivery – for your purchases from your trade supplier. Many suppliers offer the opportunity to open a trade account, which allows you a specific number of days after the invoice date in which to make payment. Depending on the credit arrangement offered, some strategic timing on your part when it comes to placing orders can make your bank balance healthier. We know of a small business that pays for its stock purchases from its supplier on the 18th of each month, the payment being for orders dispatched during the previous month. Thus, for orders dispatched by the supplier in the first few days of the month, the business enjoys some six weeks free credit. Jon, the proprietor of this one-person business, places nearly all his orders in the first week of each month.

FIT FOR PURPOSE

Your business plan marks the start of a new stage in your life. Make it look like the important document it is. Type it up and present it smartly, making sure it has a clear title page that shows your name. Protect it in a plastic folder or in some other way. Give it the professional appearance it deserves so it looks as if it's worth reading. After all, it's about something important: your business, your future.

CHAPTER 18
WHAT'S YOUR NAME?

We're aware that some of the issues we looked at in the previous chapter concerning the contents of your business plan are not the most exciting topics to deal with. However, in the interests of you and your business, it's important for you to know about them and give them some careful consideration. But we've deliberately saved for our final and very short chapter a task which many new entrepreneurs enjoy. Deciding what you will call your business.

If you will be operating as a sole trader, you've already got a name you can use – your own – if you want to. Job done. But there are reasons why you may not want to use your own name. For example, you might feel that adopting a trading name will make your new business sound more professional.

If you're devising a trading name, remember to avoid confusion with an existing business. So if you're setting up an airline, you won't be calling it Virgin Airways or anything too similar that might confuse potential customers, such as Virgon Airways. Customers and suppliers are entitled by law to know who they're dealing with, so if you set up trading as Tasty Pizzas, you must also include your own name if you are a sole trader, or the names of the partners if it is a partnership, in your business documents such as letter heading, invoices and orders for goods.

If you opt to buy a registered company, that company will already have a name. But just as you do not have to use your own name for your business, neither do you have to use the company's own name. If you buy an off-the-shelf, ready-made company, the name it comes with is likely to be unmemorable or boring. So your registered company also has the option to adopt a trading name.

In the excitement of choosing your trading name – or business name as it's also called – here are two important objectives to bear in mind. Firstly, is it a name that customers will remember? And, secondly, will it help you to stand out from the competition? Very often people who set up in business use their initials as part of their trading name, especially when the business is a partnership. The proprietors find these initials easy to remember because it's *their* initials! But *E. L. and H. N. Motors* may not be very memorable to customers.

If your business will be serving a local need and therefore not attracting customers from other areas, then using the name of the town or city in which your business is based will make it easier for potential customers to remember. This could also be an advantage for certain products or services where customers like to deal with a local supplier.

Also, note how many famous brand names are short. Sony, Ford, Sharp, Tesco, Nike spring to mind. On the other hand, if you are aiming upmarket, a long name could hint at exclusivity.

To make it easier for customers to remember your name, you could, like many other businesses, choose a name that relates to your product or service. One possible drawback is that, once you've built a reputation, the name might not be appropriate if you wish to move into another field of activity. *Heartfelt* might be a suitable name for a dating agency but not for a pig-breeding business if you later decided to go into that. On the other hand, a satisfied customer of Virgin Airways might choose to use any one of a number of other Virgin businesses. You never know, one day your business name – the one that you came up with – might become famous the world over.

POSTSCRIPT

We hope that you now have your business idea and your plan for bringing it to life.

Our experience of working with many people who wanted to set up their own business has taught us so much. So we're closing the book with the most valuable lessons we have learnt and want to pass on. These are as much to do with people as business.

We mentioned early on how research showed that many people would like to have their own business, to be their own boss. But, for most of them, it will remain just a dream. Many people come up with a business idea and then, quite properly, go through the process of evaluating that idea, along the lines we've shown you in this book. But the idea doesn't pass the evaluation test and so they come up with another idea and again, quite rightly, evaluate that. Likewise, this idea doesn't meet their criteria and they move on to another idea and evaluate that. That also turns out not to be the right one and so they come up with another idea. Then another idea...and so on. None of these ideas will work for them, they think. So they stay in their job, if they have one, or on the dole. And they never set up in business.

So beware of chasing the dream business, like them. Of forever trying to find one that is exactly right for you.

We're not, of course, suggesting that you rush ahead with the first idea that comes to mind, or without properly considering all the matters you need to consider, or taking all the advice and training you can get. But there are some people for whom it is difficult to come up with an idea that satisfies them. The list of criteria that their business idea has to satisfy is a long one. For example, the more educated you are, the longer your list is likely to be. So too, the more analytical you are. Or the more reflective you are, the more you like to think about things. If you are any – or all – of these, then beware of chasing the dream business. After all, if you set up doing something that meets, say, 19 of your list of 20 criteria, you would be gaining valuable business skills and experience and would find out whether you actually *liked* having your own business. And you could always start your dream business later, as another business, when you do find it – if you ever do.

And we understand about *risk*. The fear of risk. 'What if it doesn't work out?' One positive way of looking at this is to take the view that setting up in business today isn't such a risky option as it used to be. Because the other option, getting a job, isn't as safe as it used to be. Not so long ago, parents could say to their children that if they got a job with a bank or an insurance company, or in any one of dozens of other occupations, they'd have a job for life. But today...?

One last lesson – and this most definitely is about people. Most of the people we've worked with over the years who had this dream of setting up their own business underestimated what they were capable of achieving.

Don't be one of those people.

And one final thing for us to do:

WE WISH YOU GOOD LUCK!

APPENDIX 1

Name: ....

Record of business ideas

1. Ideas you have been considering before reading *How to Start a Business When You're Young*:

2. Ideas you can consider in the light of your *Who Am I?* questionnaire:

3. Ideas generated by:

   Chapter 1:

Chapter 2:

Chapter 3:

Chapter 4:

Chapter 5:

Chapter 6:

Chapter 7:

Chapter 8:

Chapter 9:

Chapter 10:

APPENDIX 2

Name: ....

Who am I? questionnaire

1. What sort of business would you *like* to run?

2. What work (including part-time or temporary or voluntary work) do you have experience of?

3. What skills did you acquire from the above work? And what knowledge?

4. What aspects of this work did you like?

5. a) What qualifications (if any) do you hold?

    b) What subjects have you studied?

6. a) How do you spend your leisure time? List the skills/knowledge you
       have acquired through your leisure interests:

    b) What else are you interested in?

    c) When you go to the shops, what sort of products do you like to
       look at?

7. What else are you knowledgeable about? List the skills/knowledge you have acquired through your

   a) good experiences:

   b) not-so-good experiences:

8. Any other skills?

9. What are your natural abilities (an ability you were born with, such as singing, drawing, foreign language skills, gift of the gab)?

APPENDIX 3

SOME USEFUL READING

Graham-Scott, Gini. *Let's Have a Sales Party*. Lincoln: ASJA Press, 2008

Hill, N., and Clement Stone, W. *Success Through a Positive Mental Attitude*. London: Simon & Schuster, 2007

Holden, Philip R. *Virtually Free Marketing: Harnessing the Power of the Web for Your Small Business*. London: A & C Black, 2008

Holden, Philip R., and Wilde, Nick. *Marketing and PR: Getting Customers and Keeping Them Without Breaking the Bank*. London: A & C Black, 2007

Holmes, Andrew. *Selling with Confidence: Finding and Closing Successful Deals Without Breaking the Bank*. London: A & C Black, 2008

Matthews, Dan and Martha Collier. *Starting an eBay Business For Dummies*. Indiana: Wiley Publishing Inc, 2006

Owton, Avril. *Delighting Your Customers: Delivering Excellent Customer Service Without Breaking the Bank*. London: A & C Black, 2007

Ruhe, Jan. *Let's Party: How to Succeed in Party Plan*. Cardiff: Bids Ltd, 2004

Wilson, Dan. *Make Serious Money on eBay UK*. London: Nicholas Brealey Publishing, 2007

APPENDIX 4

Action checklist

I need to do this: Deadline

1	
2	
3	
4	
5	
6	
7	
8	
9	
10	

APPENDIX 5

Some useful websites

Business Link: **www.businesslink.gov.uk**

The Prince's Trust: **www.princes-trust.org.uk**

Shell LiveWIRE programme: **www.shell-livewire.org**

National Federation of Enterprise Agencies: **www.nfea.com**

British Franchise Association: **www.british-franchise.co.uk**

The Trader: **www.thetrader.co.uk**

Federation of Small Businesses: **www.fsb.org.uk**

HM Revenue & Customs: **www.hmrc.gov.uk**

UK National Statistics, the government data website:
www.statistics.gov.uk

APPENDIX 6

MEETING COMMONPLACE NEEDS

Thousands of people make a living by running a small business that meets some commonplace need. OK, it's not an exciting or original business idea, but maybe an existing business in your area doesn't offer the best service or it doesn't have a good reputation or it's busy and there's room for a competitor.

Setting up in one of the following fields would get you into business, allowing you to gain valuable experience and earn a living until you came up with a hotter business idea. And most of these businesses will require only a relatively small capital to get started.

Bed and Breakfast
Burglar alarm sales and installations
Cakes for special occasions
Catering service for special occasions
Children's party entertainer
Chimney cleaning
Customising cars and vans
CV writing service
Cycle repair and second-hand sales
Dancing school/tuition
Dinner party catering
Dog grooming
Dog training classes
Driving tuition

Event planning
Fencing erection/repair
Fund-raising consultant
Gutter cleaning
House clearance and auction of contents
House painting
Interior decorating
Jewellery repair
Manicurist
Massage
Mobile car tune-up service
Mobile disc jockey
Mobile domestic appliance repair
Mobile hairdressing
Mobile locksmith service
Pet food supplies/delivery service
Photography for special occasions
Property-letting agency
Roof repair/replacement
Shoe repair service
Special interest weekends for hobbies (e.g. train-spotting)
Temporary help service
Training in public speaking
Upholstery/curtains/carpet cleaning
Used car inspection for car buyers
Video service for special occasions
Windscreen replacement/repair

APPENDIX 7

MEETING THE NEEDS OF BUSINESSES

Are there any businesses in your area that might require outside services? Even if there are already a number of competitors operating in a particular field, perhaps you could improve on what they are offering?

Advertising agency
Air-conditioning maintenance and repair
Blind cleaning for commercial premises
Computer repair and maintenance
Debt collection agency
Editing and proofreading service
Lunch delivery service to offices, etc.
Market research agency
Process servers serving court documents, etc.
Public relations agency
Relocation service for businesses that are moving
Sandwich delivery to offices
Supply plants for reception areas/offices
Technical writing (e.g. for instruction manuals)
Translation service
Truck and van washing
Word processing and desktop publishing

INDEX